Contents

Chapter 1

The House of Orange and Its Times

William the Silent had founded the House of Orange. William the Silent was a Lutheran and had been born into the Protestant Church in 1551. At the age of eleven he had inherited the Principality of Orange, and he was therefore obliged to conform to the Church of Rome. The paper description of the royal house was the House of Orange-Nassau. The Nassaus were of German origin, having their headquarters at the castle of Dillenburg in the Rhineland, while the principality was on the River Rhone in the South of France. Counts of Orange had ruled their lands since the age of the German Emperor Charlemagne in AD 793. In AD 1163 the Emperor Frederick Barbarossa had raised it to the status of a sovereign principality. Its prince could now wear a crown. From now on the family colours were orange and blue. Blue represented Nassau and orange the principality on the Rhone.

The royal family, despite divers lands, remained Dutch. William was a great monarch and the leading families in Europe consulted him on religious and political questions. William looked up to his sovereign, Philip II of Spain, who later in his career sent the Armada against Elizabeth I of England. The Netherlands, which now make up Holland and Belgium, were part of the Royal House of Habsburg's domains. William I played a waiting game and this had earned him the title of William the Silent. In 1567 he had to flee to Germany in order to gather forces against the ambitions of Spain and the detested Duke of Alva. He became a Calvinist, but he was assassinated in 1584. His widow was Louise de Coligny, who witnessed the death of her father, the Huguenot Admiral Coligny. Her first husband was killed during the massacre of Bartholomew's Day, 24 August 1572.

William had two sons, Maurice and Frederick Henry, who became King or Stadtholder of Holland. The princes of Orange continued the war until eventually the independence of the Netherlands was recognised in 1648. Frederick Henry's son now became William II, Stadtholder and prince. When peace eventually came, it brought with it its own difficulties. The merchants of Amsterdam were tired of high taxation, and they refused to pay their share of the cost of supporting an army. They asserted that there was no need of an army in times of peace.

William II tried to march upon Amsterdam, but the venture failed. Smitten with smallpox, William died eight days before the birth of his son, William III. He left a widow of nineteen years of age. William's mother was Mary Stuart, daughter of Charles I, a sister of Charles II and James II. She had been married to William since she was ten years of age in 1641, the year of the Irish rebellion against English rule in Ireland. The States-General now wreaked its revenge for the action of William II and deprived the House of Orange from ever becoming Stadtholder, Captain General, or Admiral General of the United Provinces.

The struggle of the Dutch against their Spanish tyrants had been effectively won by 1609 (although not finally recognised until 1648). In 1648 the Treaty of Westphalia divided the Netherlands. The south was Roman Catholic, modern Belgium remained with Spain, while the Protestant north received independence and became known as the Dutch Republic or the United Provinces. The Dutch provinces came together in the Treaty of Utrecht in 1579. The most powerful province was Holland, with its thriving cities at Amsterdam on the Zuider Zee and Rotterdam on the North Sea. Along the southern border part of the old province of Brabant was a federal territory known as the Generality, which was governed by the central government. Each province was a little republic, each with its own legislature comprised of deputies which were elected by the cities, which enjoyed a great measure of independence.

Each provincial state elected its own President or Stadtholder, but traditionally the Stadtholder was elected by five electors of the House of Orange-Nassau. The smaller provinces in the north-east, Friesland and Groningen, usually elected a member of the Nassau-Dietz line, which was descended from a brother of William the Silent. It is from this line that the present Dutch monarchy is descended, as William and Mary had no children. The Dutch parliament sat at The Hague, but could only legislate and act with the consent of every province, and now the provinces could give their consent without permission of every city.

Holland had a population of only two million compared with England's seven and half and France's nineteen million. Holland had now become a major sea power with the largest merchant fleet on the oceans and a navy which could hold its own with England, France and Spain.

Now to the politico-religious situation: The Calvinists or Presbyterians led a key role in the state, and theirs was a privileged position. Roman Catholics were in the minority, and were debarred from the major offices of state. However, they were able to practise their religion, had normal civil rights and could pursue their occupation by trade or the professions. There was a strong republican pro-French party known as the Loevestein Party, named after the prison in which Prince Maurice of Orange held some of its members. They were mainly wealthy merchants who did not like the taxes required to support the army and navy. Farmers, fishermen and the ministers of the Reformed Church tended to be strongly in sympathy with the House of Orange and its opposition to the designs of France.

William was the last descendant of William the Silent in the male line, and he was born at the Binnenhof in The Hague; his mother was just nineteen years of age, and gave birth to William on 4 November 1650. His father's dead body rested in the room next door: the bed and coffin were draped in black. Two months later William was baptised in the Groote Kerk, but his mother was ill and could not attend. She would have liked to have called the boy Charles after her father, who was executed in 1649. William II's will was not signed.

Little William's grandmother, Amalia, had her way, so he was named William Henry after his father and great-grandfather.

The court ruled that William's mother should have sole charge of his education, but his property was to be looked after by his grandmother Amalia and his uncle Frederick William, the Elector of Brandenburg, in modern Prussia. Mary of Orange did not like her people, unlike the later Mary. The two women did not get along.

There was great rivalry at sea between England and Holland and a fierce naval war had been waged between 1652 and 1654. Cromwell, as part of the peace party, stipulated that the House of Orange should be excluded from office in the Netherlands due to its Stuart connection. It was an offence to wear the Prince's colours or to sing the Orange anthem, the 'Wilhelmen'. In 1653 Charles II was in exile and a refugee in Europe. He awarded William the Order of the Garter at the age of three. Also in exile with William was his great-aunt, Elizabeth of Bohemia, the Winter Queen. Her husband accepted the Crown of Bohemia, which had led to the Thirty Years' War. She was a daughter of James I of England and a sister of Charles I. Mary, Amalia and Elizabeth all agreed that William should have a good upbringing. Formal education began at the age of five. Sir Constantine Huygens, who had been secretary to William II and his grandfather drew up a plan for the little prince. Pastor Trigland saw that William attended church twice on Sundays – a Dutch service in the morning and a French one in the afternoon. When William was eight he was presented with an important book on the deeds of the emperors, kings, etc. William had great joy when his uncle, the Elector of Brandenburg, presented him with a pony and riding breeches. All his life the young William was to have horses, riding, fresh air and country life.

At nine years of age, William's residence was moved to Leiden, noted for its resistance against the besieging Spanish Army, where William the Silent had founded a university to honour their bravery. William was now introduced to Latin, French, English and Dutch. He learnt a lot of history, geography and astronomy, and he studied the tides, for Holland was a seafaring nation. In England, Oliver Cromwell had died in September 1650, but it was not until 1660 that Charles ascended the throne of his father. The brothers, Charles and James, were invited to visit Holland before sailing to Protestant England.

William made his state journey to The Hague; his mother accompanied him in the royal coach. William sat on James's knee. Four months later the Princess Royal decided to join her royal brother. She had not seen her native land since her marriage about twenty years earlier. It was to be the last time that William was to see his mother, for she died of smallpox, which carried off Henry of Gloucester (her young brother) and then Mary. News of the dead was conveyed to William by his great-aunt, Elizabeth of Bohemia. William himself, a short time later, was stricken with asthma, headaches and fainting. He seems to have gone through a crisis in his early life that stood him in good stead later. He went on a visit to Brandenburg to visit his relations and to aid his recovery. That was to be the first time that he left Holland and his first time to go hunting – his method of relaxing. He became an addict of the chase. Here he enjoyed masculine fellowship. He captured a wild boar with some stealth from his uncle, Frederick William. After this he returned back to Leiden and his books, which he may not have liked.

Louis XIV was making trouble for the Prince, and in 1660 he occupied the Principality of Orange. He demolished its castle. However, five years later it was returned in a ruined state. Its Protestants were scattered and its churches derelict. Now William's life's work had begun. He was thirteen on 6 May 1664 and drove through the streets of The Hague in his carriage. But now he was confronted by the French Ambassador, the new envoy of Louis XIV. William was on his way to present his credentials to their High Majesties the States-General. There was no room for the coaches to pass. William decided, as a royal, not to give way to a mere ambassador. Young as he was, he found a way of expressing his feelings on behalf of his suffering subjects. The two coaches did not move, and tempers ran hot. The crowds cheered for William and shouted rude remarks at the French. Word of the situation had now reached William's grandmother; she sent for William and sent him home, and he obeyed his grandmother to go on foot.

The Reformed Churches, during the religious upheavals of 16th-century Europe, retained a revised form of the rite of confirmation. The churches at Geneva, Berne, Zurich and Basel witnessed the young prince confess his faith. He had been educated to believe in what became known as Calvinism, after the Protestant, Calvin of Geneva. His first communion was held at the age of sixteen. William's old friend, Pastor Cornelius Trigland, composed a treatise written in Latin, as a gift. It was bound in a pocket edition to be carried in a soldier's saddlebag as a blessed companion. The pious work was to be known as *The Eden of a Christian Prince*.

Psalm 101 provides a framework around which the young prince was brought up, for David is supposed to be the great example which the devout should follow. Trigland asserted that it was important for kings and princes that they should foster piety and execute judgement. Fairness was the foundation of a happy government, above all for William, for God had given the gift of future government to the Prince. All his life William believed in predestination, and that he had been called by God, for he was serving Holland. Trigland summed up future duties of William – that he was to resist all evil and to accept God's will. As Trigland was writing, the trade and colonial rivalry between England and Holland had again broken out with hostilities at sea. Holland fared badly and lost New Amsterdam, which was renamed New York after the future James II of England, a Roman Catholic, and Duke of York.

William's foremost guardian was his uncle Charles. Now an enemy of the Dutch Loevestein led by John de Witt, Charles looked favourably at William's English connections. The young prince's tutors and friends, Zuylestein and Trigland were removed with William's grandmother's consent. William was declared a child of state and commissions were appointed to supervise his upbringing. William did not like the idea, and once again he felt isolated, and that his grandmother had deserted him. However, William had become attached to the family of Count Bentinck and his wife Anna, who were not involved in politics; they enjoyed country life. The Prince's chief companion, who remained a friend for life, was their son Hans William.

The war ended in 1667, but William was to be the victim of John de Witt, who passed a Perpetual Edict abolishing the office of Stadtholder for ever.

William now took himself to Dieren for days of energetic hunting. His hopes had been dashed, but Dieren was William's favourite part of the country. Dieren lay in the province of Gelderland with a wide expanse of heath and forest. He breathed in the fresh air of pine and heather. Often in later life he would return to his home, his beloved Dieren. The most loyal of all the provinces was Zeeland, which regarded William as their noble prince. They urged him to claim his position by taking up his seat in the Assembly, for William had now come of age. He pretended that he was going to Breda, but at Walcheren Island he turned and proceeded into Middelburg with the local militia lining the route, and the country folk dressed up for the occasion and hailing William. The great bell pealed out and the celebrations continued into the night. William, now eighteen, took a greater role in government. Amongst those present was his old friend Hugens, his future secretary, who had been arranging matters behind the scenes. Breda was illuminated in his honour. William's opponents now felt that Prince William should have his wings clipped.

William had now come of age, and he took his seat on the Council of State in The Hague. He wanted to visit England to find out what the position was, and how much he could rely on his uncle, Charles II. The young Earl of Ossory, heir to the Dukedom of Ormonde of Kilkenny Castle, was said to have escorted him across the English Channel. William became a great friend of Ossory, who died some years later, but William paid homage in 1690 and made a detour from the Battle of the Boyne to visit his family home. Charles II had negotiated the secret Treaty of Dover with Louis XIV, by which France and England were to divide Holland between them. All this was unknown to Prince William. By these arrangements William would become a puppet king carrying out their instructions. Charles had agreed to convert to Roman Catholicism at a time of his choosing, whilst Louis XIV would provide Charles with a subsidy so that he would be independent of parliament. Charles was aware that William would do anything to support his position in Holland and to recover his place in the States-General. He was shocked by William's stern Protestantism, a qualitiy which did not obtain in Whitehall. The common people, though, hailed and praised William wherever he went.

William on this occasion did not meet his future wife, Mary, his cousin, and he was kept well away from her by her father, James, Duke of York (to be King James II). Charles and William remained outwardly friendly. Charles thought it wise not to let William know his plans and to leave him in the dark about the fate that would befall him as a puppet king of Louis XIV of France.

Louis was now planning his first foreign adventure with great care. By a secret treaty England had been enlisted as an ally, which was essential when considering Dutch sea power. The Eastern Provinces were to be attacked and the German principalities of Cologne and Munster across the Rhine had agreed to be French accomplices. Brandenburg was an obvious ally of Holland, but, being far off, might not be able to provide effective support. The House of Habsburg of Vienna belonged to the same family as the King of Spain and could be expected to ally itself with the Spanish Netherlands and Holland. The Habsburg Empire was in a state of decline and the Emperor was fully committed to defending his crumbling state from the Ottoman Turks, who were always advancing from the east. Vienna might be under siege. Louis realised that he had little hope of winning Spain to his cause since the Spanish Netherlands (modern Belgium) was in the front of his line of advance. The Spanish Governor now had his headquarters at Brussels and he was to prove an able leader. But Spain was not now the power it had been in an earlier age. Its territories were scattered. It ruled over a number of walled towns and cities, which boded ill for a united front against Louis XIV.

The French Army had been well trained and was equipped with the latest armaments. It was led by the former General Condé, Turenne and Luxembourg. The great builder, Vauban, had designed the defences. The French had forces made up of 25,000 horse and 86,000 elite troops. The Dutch Army had gone into decline, although the navy was in good condition. It had no captain general and the highest ranks had been filled with friends and relations. They did little more than demand their pay. Officers were permitted to live at home, so they were distant from their men.

Arms and equipment were out of date and badly maintained. The usual weapon was the awkward matchlock musket, so vulnerable to wind and weather, unlike the French flintlock. Gunpowder was sold to the French, and this made a great profit. Guns were mounted on rotten carriages. The key town was Maastricht, but it could only muster eight gunners to man its essential defences. By the autumn of 1671 the French were a real menace, and the States-General realised their mortal danger. It was too late for reform and conquest was to follow.

William of Orange was now aged twenty-one. Zeeland proposed that he should become Captain General and this was supported by all the provinces except Holland. One John de Witt held out for as long as possible, and only gave way on the appointment of a Council of Deputies, who had to approve all the actions of the Captain General.

Louis XIV of France declared war on 8 April 1672, and he set out in great splendour to join his army on the River Meuse. By May they had advanced, by passing Maastricht to gain time. The border fell with little effort. In the east the southern section fell to Louis's German allies. The weather was dry, so the French were not a victim of the weather, i.e. flooding. On 9 June 1672 Louis and his forces reached the River Rhine. He crossed it with little resistance. By the 12th, Utrecht was abandoned. Arnhem fell and Nijmegen was besieged. William had only 10,000 men against Louis's 100,000. William pitched camp just north of The Hague so that he could defend the narrow area between the North Sea and the Zuider Zee. Zeeland had almost been cut in two, and it lay to the south and managed to hold out. William looked at the problem as not being insoluble. By opening the sluices and flooding land which lay between Rotterdam and the Zuider Zee, the central citadel of the Republic would be cut off with the intensity of the floodwaters.

Five key points had to be held: Muiden, Nieuwerburg, Schoonhoven,

Dudewater and Gorinchem, since they controlled the sluices. Nuirden, near Amsterdam, was saved before the French realised its importance in maintaining the waterline. William left 3,500 men at Nieuwerburg to protect The Hague, and divided the remainder of his small forces between the other four fortresses. Now Louis XIV looked forward to a triumphal entrance into The Hague. He had a dress rehearsal at Utrecht. Mass was celebrated and the Virgin Mary venerated on the French side. Riots broke out when the Dutch realised the extent of this disaster, claiming that the government (i.e. William) had left the country unprepared for dangerous situations.

De Witt now sought surrender to Louis. He was given an ultimatum demanding the southern part of the Republic, the River Rhine, as well as four cities. All the Republic's colonies were to be handed over to Louis, and Roman Catholic priests were to be paid out of public funds. The terms were generous and the Dutch were to present Louis each year with a gold medal expressing their thanks for French clemency. Louis did not like William, and showed his contempt of him. The Principality of Orange was occupied and its defences destroyed. All had seemed lost and John de Witt sent his envoy, de Groot, back to accept French terms, but now events got out of control.

The common people blamed the situation on the ruling classes, particularly the Grand Pensionary, John de Witt. It was rumoured that the armed peasants were descending upon The Hague. The de Witts had taken refuge in the prison, but the guns were not in a position to save them. They were dragged out into the street and murdered. William at once went to The Hague, where he heard of the outrage. William found that only half of The Hague was in the control of his men, and there was nothing left to be done except to save what was left of the principality. The French terms were rejected and William was restored to all the offices of state held by his ancestors. William chose Gaspar Fagel to replace de Witt, and then appointed Waldeck as Field Marshal of the army.

By June the strength of the Dutch Army had been realised at 9,000 men, but by September it had been expanded to 30,000. Only experience could turn it into a reliable force. William campaigned in the wet of winter weather against Louis. The main problem was that the French troops might attack over the ice when the water was frozen solid. On 27 December people had been butchered and burnt, and Luxembourg managed to reach the villages of Bodegraven and Zwammerden. Only a nine-month-old child was left alive. By now a great thaw set in. Luxembourg was lucky to make his way back to Utrecht, although most of his men lay dead. William was busy rebuilding his butchered forces, and he disciplined the army by being fair but firm. He saw to it that the soldiers were paid promptly and that their welfare was looked after in field hospitals; he set an example for his men by always being in the thick of battle. The States-General was not keen on William's enthusiasm, and they begged him to take more care of his person. He galloped into the field wearing his star and blue sash of the Garter, and this made him an enemy target, but he made no efforts to protect himself.

The Emperor of Austria now, in 1673, declared war on France and this was in William's favour. The campaign season had now opened again. On 7 June Admirals de Ruyter and van Tromp defeated the combined fleets of France and England. This prompted Charles II to disengage from the war, preventing an invasion of Holland from the sea. On 12 August William visited his fleet to show his appreciation. He was warmly received.

Victory at sea prompted Spain at last to take the field, and up to now it had acted in the defensive role. This allowed William room to move. In September he struck south to Amsterdam, recapturing Naarden at the southern edge of the Zuider Zee, and he reunited his country in the face of France. It was his first victory, which brought him great prestige. Now he moved against Louis's German forces; the Electors of Cologne and Munster could now be separated from the main French forces. But the season for warfare was now drawing to a close. He secretly led 9,500 Dutch and 3,000 Spanish troops into the German Rhineland. He took the great fortress of Koblenz, which lay at the junction between the Rhine and the Moselle. Now he led a night attack in person on the city of Bonn, which surrendered in November. The German force withdrew from Dutch territory. The Dutch Republic now seemed a united country.

1674 saw an end to the war with England. The year opened with the Treaty of Westminster. Charles II's position was now becoming perilous and he was glad to bring this unpopular war to an end. Cologne and Munster also retreated, leaving France to fight against Holland, Spain, Austria and Brandenburg. The French now evacuated the remainder of the Dutch territory in the province of Utrecht, which two years earlier had failed to fight in its own defence. The people watched in silence as Louis's troops retreated. William of Orange's standard appeared on the highest tower, bells rang out and the people headed for the churches and cathedrals. William was almost the only monarch in Europe who succeeded in opposing the will of France.

Only the Dutch towns remained in Louis's hands. But the remainder of the war would not be fought outside the Spanish Netherlands. Louis would have been pleased if he could sign a peace treaty with William. William did not desert his allies or abandon them to sign a separate treaty. He looked to the future and the day when Holland would be a safe country to live in, and friends and allies were important too. To this cause he dedicated the rest of his life. A general battle had to be avoided, so through the summer of 1674 William and Condé marched and countermarched, sizing up each other but making no move. The allies in August had advanced into the heart of the Spanish Netherlands, with Spain at the head, the Dutch in the centre and the Austrians in the rear. But the Spanish lost their way not far from the town of Mons. They blundered into the French whilst making an advance in the narrow defile at Seneffe. Condé, in an experiment, did not turn up his nose at taking advantage of William's enemies. He attacked and routed the vanguard, sending the Spanish into disarray. After two years at war, the Dutch and William rested secure, and William in his first major battle restored order out of chaos.

Long and bloody was the battle, and it continued into the night; by dawn the French had retired and left William and his allies in possession of the field. Some 7,000 men on both sides lay dead, wounded, or made prisoner. But the French claimed victory as they had captured so many Spanish standards. It was Condé's last battle and he had been greatly impressed by the young William. Grave was captured in October after a two-month siege. The French had put up an admirable defence, and he ordered the garrison to march out with all the honours of war. The work of restoration could now begin, repairing the damage done by Louis XIV and by the general flooding.

William wanted to be Stadtholder of the Province of the Republic, his lifelong ambition to regain an hereditary title in the male line. The principality offered the Prince the sovereignty of their realm, but William declined this offer with regret. Flanders was the cockpit of Europe and here the war dragged on for another four years. The Duke of Luxembourg and William persisted in a challenge without result. Behind the scenes the nations had started to bring about peace. Mons was under siege in 1678, and William started to march for its relief. The Duke of Luxembourg, whose headquarters were the small town and abbey of St Denis, was well prepared for a fight. Now William freed a contingent of British troops in Dutch pay – three Scots, two English and one Irish regiment, the latter being under the command of Thomas Butler, Earl of Ossory.

The battle was waged well into the night like the battle of Seneffe. By morning the French had gone, leaving behind their dead, wounded, supplies and tents. It was now that an attempt was made upon William's life. His cousin, Henry Nassau, seeing a Frenchman levelling a pistol at the Stadtholder, shot the French horseman dead. Peace had been signed at last, and Luxembourg knew this before the battle had begun – he wanted the defeat of William, and Mons would fall into the Duke's hands before the treaty could be ratified. This was the Treaty of Nijmegen, and, despite France's superiority, the battle ended in the defeat of Louis XIV. The United Provinces had believed in 'no surrender' and stood firm, along with the romantic figure of the young prince, who had led their armies into battle. The soldiers of William marched home, but the Prince took off a few days later for hunting, to relax. France returned Lorraine to its duke, Maastricht to Holland, and now William regained the Principality of Orange.

Now, in 1674, after peace had been signed with England – but not with France – Sir William Temple, an old friend of the Dutch people, returned to The Hague as English Ambassador. A great friendship had developed between Sir William and Prince William, and they were completely open and honest with each other. As a friend of William, Sir William sought his advice, and he became a happily married man in April 1676. William himself wanted to wed, but his bride would have to be a royal or of princely rank, a Protestant, and a person acceptable to the States and worthy of winning the allegiance of the Dutch people. Princess Mary Stuart was considered a good match for such a Protestant potentate. She was the eldest daughter of his uncle, the Duke of York. Sir William said that it was a wise match.

William now wrote letters to his uncle seeking permission to visit England. He gave the letter to Lady Temple, who was shortly to depart for England. William went back to his army post and eighteen months were to pass before he could undertake the expedition. It eventually took place in the autumn of 1677. Mary was only sixteen years of age, while the Prince was twenty-seven. Mary's mother, Anne Hyde, had died in 1671 when Mary was only nine years of age. Her father married again in 1673 to the Italian princess, Mary Beatrice Modena. King Charles was pleased with his brother's second marriage, for the first had been unpopular with the general public. Mary of Modena liked her step-daughters, Mary and Anne, who were not much younger than she was.

Mary was now a very pretty girl with natural gifts and quick wits; she was gentle and kind. She was tall, being five foot eleven inches in height. She had been carefully trained in etiquette. She had received a mainly religious education. She was well versed in the scriptures and Anglican doctrine by her tutor. She had been confirmed, when she was twelve years of age, by the Bishop of London, Henry Compton, and she was strictly devout.

Meanwhile, William had landed at Harwich and was taken to Newmarket where he could watch the races. King Charles was anxious to involve him in state affairs, but William did not like the idea until he met Mary at London. Mary was charming, so he thought, and he made up his mind immediately to marry her. He asked Charles for Mary's hand. Charles was pleased, and, although Mary's father was a Catholic, James believed in the divine right of kings, and he bowed to his brother's wishes. Mary, to begin with, had little knowledge that she was to be married to William of Orange, and, when told, she wept for the whole day – she would be taken away from the English court to be William's wife in

Holland, which might mean that she was bending to a Republic's will and compromising with Dissenters. She was ignorant of Dutch.

The marriage was celebrated on the evening of William's birthday, 4 November, at St James's Palace, in Mary's bedchamber, by Dr Compton. By James's request the bride was given away by the King. The Queen was not present for she disapproved of the marriage. Anne was seriously ill with suspected smallpox, and this prevented Mary from saying farewell to her sister. The celebration at court went on for a fortnight; the entire realm from Edinburgh to London was rejoicing with the ringing of bells.

At last William and Mary set out for Holland on 5 November, but bad weather held them up, and it was not until 29 November that the ship could drop anchor in the port of Ter Heyde. The Dutch celebrations could now begin. William was to find much happiness in his marriage to Mary. Like most marriages it had its low moments, when Mary was still a young girl at school, and when William was involved with the war with Louis XIV. In 1678 Mary suffered a miscarriage, followed by two false pregnancies. It seems that the miscarriage was due to Mary making a long journey to meet William at Breda, and this may have caused permanent damage, for she never conceived again.

Gradually the marriage of William and Mary was successful and they started to love one another; they followed the simple Calvinist faith and a high standard of morals. Both preferred country houses to life at The Hague. Mary's favourite house was Honselaersdijk, only seven miles from The Hague, and attractively situated. Mary became as popular with the Dutch as her husband was. Mary loved the open countryside and the country houses, which were very clean. She shared William's passion for architecture, interior decoration and, above all, gardens. William had plans for a great new palace at Het Loo, near Dieren, William's favourite retreat, with gardens after the French style, but Mary was never to see this completed for she left Holland in 1689, never to return. During the long years of her marriage, William flirted with one of Mary's ladies, the intelligent and witty Elizabeth Villiers. William seemed to be displeased at the marriage. William intercepted letters between Mary's chaplain and the English Ambassador. Mary said that he had done everything possible before God so that they should remain happily married. Mary burst into tears and threw herself into William's arms. Most authorities agree that the relationship between Mary and William was more spiritual than physical. But as the years went on the love of William for Mary blossomed. When he was away on his campaigns, Mary was always worried that he might not return alive. She yearned for his return after a campaign.

The Treaty of Nijmegen of 1678 was unsatisfactory, and William's patience was tried. He seems to have been the only ruler who saw danger before him. Louis XIV was trying to take over Europe. Louis was occupied in organising tens of thousands of men, who had been labouring for years in the building of the great palace of Versailles. It was to be the greatest palace in Europe, but it was cold and draughty in winter and huge fires filled the rooms with smoke.

Charles II was William's uncle, and William made his third visit to England in July 1681. Mary was not able to accompany him, but the after-effects of her marriage had left her with little strength, and prevented her from travelling. Charles was having trouble with the English parliament, which now had a Whig (Liberal) majority, but it was opposed to James, Duke of York. James had been converted to Roman Catholicism, and was excluded from inheriting the throne from Charles II. Charles, to frustrate the Whigs, dissolved parliament, which did not meet again during his reign. As a result of this, England had to rely on French subsidies. Upon his visit to the English court, William found out that the Whigs were not interested in Louis XIV or the threat to Europe. Both Charles and James were jealous of the popularity of the young William of Orange. Charles forbade him to attend a dinner given by the Lord Mayor of London. James considered going into honourable exile, for he might be the victim of violence. Some of the Whigs were now driven to despair and were involved in the plot of 1683 to overthrow Charles II in favour of the Duke of Monmouth, who himself had to flee to Holland and then to Brussels. In 1682 Louis XIV witnessed the repair of the Dutch defences of the Orange Principality, and this would threaten French frontiers. Louis ordered the army to invade the Prince's little state, with orders to demolish its defences and trouble all those who questioned the position of Louis XIV.

William was very angry with Louis, and his friends urged him to take his time and prayed that he would not die before he had the means to let Louis know what it meant to be a Prince of Orange. French troops started to storm Luxembourg, which belonged to Spain, and by treaty William was obliged to help the people of the Duchy. William asked the States to levy 16,000 men, half of which should be for the province of Holland. The rich merchants were opposed to his plans, and behind William's back they were carrying on negotiations with the French Ambassador, le Comte d'Avaux, who was later to play a leading role in the Irish siege of the city of Londonderry in 1689. William now intercepted the envoy's courier, and stole his papers. He now presented the States-General with the incriminating letters and forced two of the guilty back to Holland. He was still defensive in the face of French aggression. Louis seized Strasbourg on the Rhine in the Emperor's domain in 1684, but the Turks were at the gates of Vienna, so he was able to resist. Luxembourg fell. The Spanish and Dutch allies submitted to the terms of the Treaty of Ratisbon, by which Louis XIV agreed to a twenty-year truce, a truce which no one trusted.

Louis now turned his own Protestant supporters by revoking the Edict of Nantes, which had granted some toleration to the Huguenots. They hated the Mass, and were forced to attend. Those who resisted were sent to the galleys. In the years that followed hundreds of thousands left for England, Holland and Prussia, bringing with them their skills and a hatred of Roman Catholicism.

Charles II died in 1685 and his brother James ascended the throne. He was to force the Spanish to expel his illegitimate nephew, the Duke of Monmouth, from Brussels, so that he could return to Holland, but William gave him no encouragement. Some of William's enemies in Amsterdam helped the Duke of Monmouth to get together an expedition, and he sailed for England in June. He landed on the south coast at Lyme Regis in Dorset, and gathered together an army of puritan peasants and artisans. On 6 July at Sedgemoor in Somerset his troops were cut to pieces by regular troops under John Churchill and Percy Kirke. The Duke was executed and hundreds of his supporters were hanged or sold into slavery by the notorious Judge Jeffreys.

Many English Protestants began to arrive in Holland, amongst them the Scots Episcopalian clergyman, Dr Gilbert Burnet. He was a friend of the executed Duke of Argyll and was the author of *A History of the Reformation*. He got on well with William, to great surprise, and had much influence on Queen Mary, who could not make up her mind whether to support her father or her husband. The Whig interpretation of events prevailed. She could see her position more clearly. It was possible that she might succeed to the English throne, being heir presumptive, and that William would automatically become King. The law might dictate otherwise. Mary told William that the law of God was greater than the law of England. She was resolved to keep the commandment that wives should obey their husbands and husbands should love their wives.

In November 1686 James II sent William Penn, the Quaker, to ask William and Mary to support his campaign for the repeal of the penal laws and Test Acts. James wanted to get rid of the law affecting Roman Catholics. William Penn was a sincere man that could not see through James's policies and ambitions. William was for the freedom of religious worship according to conscience. James wanted to repeal the Test Acts (which forbade Roman Catholics from holding civil or military office under the Crown). James did not like William's position, but he went ahead with his plans. He defied public opinion and the law by which Roman Catholics could not sit in the Privy Council. Also, he established an Ecclesiastical Commission to control appointments in the Church of England. Now, in October 1686, Richard Talbot was created Earl of Tyrconnel, and he was appointed Lord Lieutenant of Ireland.

In early 1687, Dijkvelt was appointed Ambassador to England in the

Dutch Republic, with instructions to keep William informed about James II's position and to gauge the mood of the country. James now appointed Ignatius White as Ambassador to the Dutch Republic, with instructions to find out how William stood in regard to developments in England. The King now tried to woo his daughter to the Catholic faith. She had mentioned to the Dutch Ambassador that she had often wondered what had brought about her father's conversion to Roman Catholicism. James said that it was the doctrine of papal infallibility that had won him over, and he wrote a long letter to his daughter describing his position. He enclosed a book for her to read, and waited for an answer. Mary, to everyone's surprise, wrote a lengthy reply. She said that she was not impressed by the book of *Reflections and Differences in Religion*. She said that James did not expect her to change her religious views.

The first breach between William and James II came in January 1688. William refused to appoint Roman Catholics to serve with the six English and Scottish foot regiments in the Dutch service. James wanted their recall. William was within his legal rights in refusing but it was only invoked in time of war between England and Holland. He allowed some soldiers to go home if they wanted to, and many, mainly Roman Catholics, did so. The Dutch Ambassador to the English court had carried out his obligations very well. He had asked for the opinion of the Tory Earls of Banby and Nottingham. Also, he had been in contact with the Bishop of London, Sir Henry Compton, who had been suspended from his office because of a sermon he had preached about Reformation doctrine. Admiral Arthur Herbert was also dismissed for his part in refusing James II's designs. Major General John Churchill had also been approached. His wife had great influence over Princess Anne, now married to George of Denmark. The Ambassador, Dijkvelt, returned to The Hague with letters from these well-known men. He was succeeded as envoy by William's cousin, Zuylestein, who continued the contacts with yet more letters.

James was near the climax of his reign. He issued a second Declaration of Indulgence, which claimed to bypass Acts of Parliament. Thus it was ordered that the Declaration should be read in all parish churches on two successive Sundays in May and June. William Sancroft, Archbishop of Canterbury, summoned his bishops for an urgent meeting at London, but only seven were able to make the date. A petition was published and had the signature of all except the Archbishop of Canterbury, who was suspended from office. Those who were put up for trial were suspended from office. Those who were part of the trials – the Archbishop himself, Francis Turner (Ely), William Lloyd (St Asaph), Thomas Ken (Bath and Wells), John Lake (Chichester), Jonathan Trelawney (Bristol) and Thomas White (Peterborough). Now, on 10 June 1688, before the case could be heard, a son was born to James II and Mary of Modena (the little boy being heir to the throne). Extreme Protestants proclaimed that this was a time to take up the Protestant cause and not to subject England to the Pope's rule. At this moment James II moved his troops, almost entirely Roman Catholic, from Dublin to Chester. They marched across England and camped on the outskirts of London on Hounslow Heath.

On 29 June the trial of the seven bishops was held at Westminster Hall. England held its breath until the jury eventually returned a verdict of 'not guilty'. That night London decided to contact The Hague, which was not very important for the future liberty of James's subjects. William would not let himself be influenced by professions of goodwill, but he wanted the ear of the rich and powerful men. The request to Holland was that it should support all efforts to control the Crown for a Protestant England. Three had signed for the Whigs. The Church was represented by Sir Henry Compton. It was left to Herbert to discuss practical measures with William, i.e. the best situations for landing his troops. William proceeded with great enthusiasm, and new ships were fitted out. Troops from numerous parts of Protestant Europe were raised and assembled at a great camp near Nijmegen to combat French threats to Cologne. Arms, ammunition, horses and waggons, food and fodder were stockpiled. Boats ferried portable bridges, a mobile smith and a printing press. The invitation had warned that his troops should bring some engineers with them.

Marshal Schomberg was appointed second in command, which brought great experience to William's army in the way of language. Waldeck was to take charge of home defence, with a mainly German Army. D'Avaux was suspicious. By August he was sending reports to the French court that the English were preparing for war. More information came to light during James's reign, but this was discarded as it was offered at the wrong time. Edward Russell now arrived at Het Loo with the latest men from England, along with Henry Sidney and Shrewsbury. They had brought with them £3,000 in cash. William by now had won the support of his cousin (Frederick, Elector of Brandenburg), the Elector of Saxony, and other German princes. D'Avaux's warnings began to be heeded, and Louis XIV issued a declaration that any war waged against England would be regarded as a declaration of war against France. James denied the rumour that the secret Treaty of Dover had been removed and condemned Louis's right to intervene. Louis made no more efforts to help. Louis considered that William should not leave Holland until he was well protected.

It was Louis that solved William's dilemma. In the spring of 1688 the Archbishop of Cologne, one of Louis's mentors, died. He had regarded the River Rhine as his frontier and he had wanted his armed muster assembled in that sensitive area. All were agreed (from the Emperor to Pope Innocent XI) that Prince Clement of Bavaria should succeed to the

Archbishopric. His troops in Flanders marched to the Rhineland in order to attack the fortress of Philipsburg. The Emperor defended himself against the Turks at Belgrade, and relieved Vienna. Peace was made in the east, and he was able to lead his forces to deal with this fresh attack. Louis depended upon the neutrality of England, and he wasted no time in being engaged in a long drawn-out war. But William was able to land in England – Louis was heavily engaged in a war of his own making. He also made a mistake by threatening the States-General of the Dutch Republic and warning them about making allies that would be in England's favour. Louis's actions only made William's supporters more determined to establish a Calvinist position.

William now took leave of the States on 16 October, leaving Mary in their care and thanking them for their loyalty. William said to a sad Mary that if he did not return from the wars, that she was to marry again. The fleet set sail on the 20th. It was made up of 200 transport ships and fifty warships, but a fierce storm stood in their way and William had to fight his way back to port with the loss of one ship and a great many horses. In both England and Holland, William's supporters sat on the edge of their chairs. Now a wind started to blow and once more William's armada hoisted sail and made its way into the North Sea. The plan had been to head north, where his supporters were ready to rise, but the weather might only hold good until nightfall. A good wind blew, and William yielded and kept the English fleet at Dartmouth, firmly bottled up in the Thames Estuary. Now they headed westwards. The fleet was safely through the Straits of Dover by 3 November. William's banners streamed out. On Sunday 4 November, William's birthday, the white cliffs of Dover were visible, but still the fleet held its course, until the wind changed and a fresh breeze sprang up from the south, which carried William safely into Torbay in Devon. William stepped ashore at the fishing village of Brixham with sixty boats conveying 15,000 troops to land later that afternoon. As William turned to his friend, Burnet, he said, "What so you think of predestination now, Doctor?" Praise was given to God for the safe landing and for the coming campaign against the papish James II. They sang the 118th Psalm. A strong wind blew the following day from the west, turning William back and bringing four days of rain, whilst the army made its way to Exeter, the first important town, and entered with full pomp and ceremony.

The common people gave William's army a great reception, but the bishops and their dignitaries fled. A service was held in the cathedral, and William's declaration was read out. It outlined in great detail James's infringement of their civil and religious liberties by arbitrary power. Parliament was encouraged to make new laws. William renounced all thought of conquest, and undertook to return with his English Army as soon as the nation was delivered from James's tyranny. He halted at Exeter for about two weeks to allow Englishmen to join the crusade against popery. At Burnet's suggestion an association was formed and a declaration drawn up to be signed by its members pledging them to support France and one another until the object of the declaration could be achieved.

Exeter was some distance away in the West Country, where no one would have expected a landing, and the people remembered the bloody events only three years previously. The response was slow at first, but it soon became a flood. The Earl of Bath, Edmund Seymour, arrived at the scene. Lord Delamare took Chester for William. Danby seized York and Devonshire occupied Nottingham.

James tried to reverse all his policies and talked of recalling parliament. He set out to join his forces at Salisbury and arrived there on 19 November before William continued his march on London. On the 23rd, James lost his nerve and headed back to the capital, which prompted Churchill, Kirke and Grafton to cross over to William's side. William advanced on Hungerford, where he met James's commissioners and stated his terms: both armies were to remain a distance from London, a free parliament was to be called, to be attended by both William and James, Roman Catholics illegally appointed to positions were to be dismissed and all proclamations against William revoked.

James would have nothing to do with the terms. He had now sent his wife and son off to Louis XIV, and tried to follow them in December. He was stopped at Sheerness, for his ship had missed the tide, and he was brought back to London, which embarrassed William. James was now given a second opportunity to escape, and he finally sailed for France on 3 December 1688. It was now proposed to elect a free parliament without delay, and until there was a sovereign it was styled a convention, meeting on 22 June 1689. The House of Commons was predominantly Whig, and declared that James had broken the original contract between King and people, for there were subversions to the fundamental laws, and now the throne was vacant. The House of Lords, predominantly Tory, rejected by two votes a proposal for a regency. In their view the Crown had already approached Mary. Mary said that she would not become Queen until William was made King. On 6 February, the House of Lords backed down and both houses offered the Crown to William and Mary jointly. At the moment Mary was in Holland, torn between William and her father, James II, and feeling guilty about his humiliation. She had now to join her husband in England, but she was sad about parting, for she would never see her Dutch subjects again. She worshipped and prayed, and arrived in England on 11 February. On the 13th the Declaration of Rights was read by the joint houses: William and Mary were offered the throne.

The convention could now become a parliament and the Declaration of Rights eventually became the Bill of Rights. This was the famous cornerstone of our liberties, covering many things. The Protestant succession of a monarch was assumed along with the position of the army, the judges, and the exclusive right of parliament to raise taxes. However, William and Mary were dependent upon parliament for money, and that had now altered the position of the monarchy.

The Bill of Rights brought religious toleration, which ended the Church of England's legal monopoly of the nation's religious rights south of the border. Scotland had its own convention, which established Presbyterian government. The Bill of Rights safeguarded all aspects of Britain's life, and condemned those who would not cooperate with William and Mary before the Whitehall gates, and declared that the great struggle was over concerning the right of William to be monarch along with his wife.

Chapter 2

Before the Battle of the Boyne

60,000 men fought at the Battle of the Boyne, 1,690 greater than that of any other battle in Ireland and Britain. Every year on 12 July the Protestants of Ulster march in defiance of the Catholics in many places in Northern Ireland. The Battle of the Boyne symbolised the violence of the religious and political conflict. The King, William of Orange, and James II contended with each other for the crown of England, Scotland and Ireland. Upon the fate of this battle – it is claimed – rested the future peace and progress in Europe, for Louis XIV, as we have seen, had tried to divide Protestants and Catholics in Ireland. The importance of the Battle of the Boyne has been set out by many historians and politicians, especially those who understand military history. To fight the Battle of the Boyne, money had to be raised as well as supplies and troops; all were essential so that the armies could fight. Britain was a very wealthy country and there was a steady flow of revenue to the Crown. Ireland had a basically cashless, agrarian economy. Even if William had lost the Battle of the Boyne, there was still plenty of Pope-hatred to aggravate matters. The Boyne was not, some say, as decisive as the siege of Aughrim a year later, where there was much bloodshed. This brought about the end of resistance to revolt in Ireland. William had not invaded Ulster in the last week of 1688 because of religious reasons. William claimed that there had been a Glorious Revolution because it was bloodless. James II was William's uncle and father-in-law.

William of Orange represented the Grand Alliance, whereby every state was fighting Louis XIV's France for control in Europe. William had beaten the French, and the Alliance was officially over. Ireland was to be James's stepping stone to power in London, and when he fought at the Boyne he did so with many allies. Over a third of the soldiers that fought at the Boyne came from Europe. If James had managed to kill William at the Boyne, then his path would be open to a long march to

London to recover his crown. William was afraid that James would win the war. But James had lost his nerve and there had been nerves at the court amongst the turncoats that had supported James and then supported dethronement. He had gone into exile, much to the relief of William of Orange.

Louis XIV had shipped 6,000 troops to Ireland and these were utilised at the Boyne. The French king regarded Ireland as a good ground for recruitment for an attack against England. But this came to an end. Now French warships dominated the seas around Ireland. The allies feared that there might be a restoration of James, but history has proven that the Boyne was only an isolated incident and was overshadowed by the French fleet. There was much celebration when the people saw their Catholic king leave for the Continent, and all were now gathered around William. Protestants claimed that God had given them victory and James and the Virgin Mary were relegated to the history books. James was regarded as a coward. There was to be a complete change in government in Ireland. Anglicans could live in peace, along with the Presbyterians in the province.

At the time of the battle there were various conclusions to be drawn. Some thought that it was a rout rather than a battle. There was a concentration of troops in a confined area. The Boyne was a battle between James II and William III, fighting from dawn to dusk, skirmishing throughout a long hot day across eighteen square miles of cornfields, hamlets, hills and river. The Boyne was not very bloody in comparison to other battles on land or on the seas. The most important facets of any battle are morale, the type of weapons used, and the ground it is fought over. A number of tactical changes had taken place between the mid-1680s and the mid-1690s. The allied army had undergone modernisation, but not so the French–Irish Army. The Battle of the Boyne was fought between soldiers that marched in cadenced steps, so presenting a column as they went into battle. Traditional battles could take anything up to three or four days.

Modern historians view the Battle of the Boyne as being tactically indecisive. The armies of James and William found it hard to strike out for victory. The English and the Protestants of Ulster were confident that England would defeat James II and confine Louis XIV to the Continent, for he had eyes to usurp the English throne and send William back to Holland.

Facts are hard to come by regarding the positions of the various forces on both sides and most accounts vary regarding the position in Ireland. An account of the allied army crossing Oldbridge on the River Boyne demands an understanding of the uses of the sword and bayonet as opposed to the smooth-bore muskets; also the various kinds of muskets and firing techniques. The cavalry were held in reverse under volley fire and used their swords when pursuing those running away from the scene of the battle in panic.

James II had gone against the counsels of history in trying to impose Roman Catholicism and absolutism in Britain, so the revolution that overthrew the Catholic king was, as far as and the Protestants were concerned, a good one. Richard Bagwell's three-volume *Ireland under the Stuarts,* downplays the importance of the Boyne, but he emphasises that the effect was enormous. Others have seen that the Boyne was not an heroic Protestant victory but represents action by a heavily entangled army that inflicted heavy losses. The question is whether James's army might have made a better showing, and whether the Boyne position was tenable; also whether the Jacobites were up to scratch. William did not fail to take advantage of his superior numbers and equipment. Were his military tactics sound, and why did James flee with an army after only small losses?

The diary of Constantine Huygens records that King William had two secretaries. William kept them in the dark as far as his plans were concerned, for one of the secretaries was a gossip. The diary contains much camp rumour and a lot of trivia. William craved chocolate and spent the morning of the battle drinking raspberry syrup with the Brandenburg envoy in his tent. The public were kept informed about the progress of events, and pamphlets were published in the Netherlands. Fewer accounts of the battle exist on the Jacobite side. Of these more than one features in *A Light to the Blind*, written by an Irishman.

The Gaels did not like the accession of James I to the throne in 1603. They loathed him, but Charles I was hoping to obtain Irish help during the civil war of 1642–53. This help never materialised, but the Irish eventually fought for Charles II in the latter stages of the wars. Scots conventions and Irish Catholics were targeted for discrimination. Charles I had yearly openly detested the presence of Presbyterians: "For my part, rebel to rebel, I had rather trust a papist rebel than a Presbyterian one."

Oliver Cromwell had reconquered Ireland in 1649–53. The 1641 rising had occurred and there was barbarism on both sides, but these reports may be exaggerated. There was to be an ethnic cleansing in Ireland of the natives, for they were to be sent to Connaught in the west of Ireland, to the rough and poor lands. Cromwell's Protectorate soon punished the leadership rather than the masses by confiscating native Irish land in order to pay the arrears due to the troopers. In an agrarian society the ownership of land meant power. When Charles II was restored, the land settlement of 1663–65 fell short of expectations. The proportion of land ownership rose back to little more than 22 per cent, compared to a pre-war figure of 60 per cent. The Catholics were bitter, for they had lost their lands in supporting King Charles.

That the Catholics lost their position in Ireland is due to the disunity amongst themselves. The old English had won over the Gaelic Irish, and a Confederate party sprang up amongst those who wished to curtail the power of England. The Catholics wanted some of their old lands back and no further plantations. The fault line was not ethnic, and by 1640 the Catholic elite had been intermarried, and family connections were the lifeblood of the Antrim plantation. This was a situation that still obtained after the Restoration. Church and laity squabbled over a suitable declaration that would support British imperial power in the island. This idea was something of a turning point. Anti-Jacobite opinion was, perhaps, due to the policies of Richard Talbot, later to become Lord Deputy of Ireland under James II. He went into exile.

The surviving pattern of Catholic land ownership was tactically important. Most Catholic military units were seigneurial, and they were led by notables using their position with the King to attract followers. In 1688 there existed forty-three Jacobite infantry; all but seven were reorganised – Creegh, Moore, Dorrington, Tyrone, Grand Prior, Boisseleau and Hamilton. Most of the captains were linked to their colours by clientship or by land dependency. The remainder of the captains had County Cavan surnames, such as Smith and Brady, or surnames from adjacent counties, from Monaghan and Westmeath.

James Butler the Duke of Ormonde, Charles II's Governor of Ireland, favoured his Catholic relations on the land-restoration scramble. He possessed a significant domain in the south of the country. There was a considerable Catholic population of landowners in Galway and Mayo – on land set aside for Catholics who had lost their land by other means. Ulick Burke had followed Butler in his policies throughout the 1640s. So too had Viscount Theobald Costello and the 2nd Earl of Westmeath. They had estates in Mayo, Roscommon, and Westmeath, which extended the growth of Catholic landownership. This can be compared to the Pale of medieval origin around Dublin. It was through this land that the River Boyne flowed. Richard Talbot had considerable interest in the status quo, for he was a confidant of James II, the Catholic king. Catholic lands were to be returned before the Court of Claims was suspended in 1665. The position in North Antrim, where the MacDonnells held sway, was important, for here Randal MacDonnell, 2nd Earl of Antrim, regained his estates despite a record of hostility towards Ormonde.

Names chosen in 17th-century Ireland are extremely difficult to understand. The term 'British' is a little out of place, for Ireland was a separate kingdom from that of Scotland, England and Wales. The term 'Irish Protestant' was not adopted by the ruling classes, and this was a situation that obtained for fifty years. The pre-1640 or old Protestant settlers dominated the planters' or colonisers' interest: Only the MPs in the Restoration parliament belonged to the Cromwellian interest.

The basis of Protestant power was the possession of land, access to office and, eventually, trade. The Protestant population had increased in Restoration Ireland, reflecting the fall in the native Irish population. There were the Cromwellian land policies to be taken into account, and there were large numbers of Protestants waiting to take up land in Ireland, 10–20 per cent of the population. The higher estimate would have obtained with a large Scots presence. Protestants had become the governing power in great numbers on the land. At the outbreak of the Jacobite wars Ireland had a total population of just under two million. They would be hostile to any Irish Catholic regime. It was doubtful if they could organise themselves into any kind of resistance, but the attempt to succeed depended upon demography. There were centres of armed resistance – the Laggan region of north-east Donegal, abutting the city of Londonderry, but excluding Inishowen and East Ulster (North Down, South and Mid-Antrim). There was a centre of resistance at Enniskillen in County Fermanagh. The walled town of Bandon served as a place of refuge in West Cork. Dublin had Ireland's greatest concentration of Irish Protestants: many had immigrated to the 'fair city' and its population had recovered from wartime conditions. It grew rapidly from the mid-1650s, so that by 1685 it contained 45,000 people, about two thirds of them Protestant. Her nearest rival was Cork, numbering 18,000 in 1706, but slightly less in the late 1680s. Before the accession of the Catholic James II, both Protestants and Catholics existed side by side in a state of continual antipathy. The Catholics had been stripped of their economic and political power with a fall in the proportion of Catholic landownership.

Chapter 3

James II and the Aftermath of the Glorious Revolution

The Battle of the Boyne has become a political symbol in Northern Ireland. The battle was fought at the River Boyne on 12 July 1690. It has been claimed that this battle was as important as that in any other country in the 17th century. It was not of any great political significance, even though it ended with the Catholic James II's flight to the court of Louis XIV of France. The Jacobite losses were not great. The bulk of them retreated in an orderly manner, but regrouped in the west of the country at Limerick where they held out against William III for another twelve months.

The Battle of Aughrim was, however, to be the decisive victory of the Irish wars. It was disastrous for the Jacobite supporters, and it was to be another hundred years before an Irish Army took the field against Jacobitism. How then did the Battle of Aughrim live on in history? It has left an unending impression on the Irish nation. Each year on 12 July, Ulster Protestants celebrate the overthrow of James II in song, poems, pious music and dancing. It was said that William of Orange and his immortals humbled the Pope and the papacy at the River Boyne. The cry heralded in an era of peace with the flight of James, and the victory of William brought an era of civil and religious liberty from anti-Catholic oppression.

It was eight o'clock in the evening until three o'clock in the afternoon when the four 6-pounder guns fired, backed up by four great howitzers. The gunners of William Henry of Orange, William III of England, were exhausted. They had fired shots across the Boyne, which separated them from the camp of the deposed James II. The gunners were based about three hundred yards away from the banks of the River Boyne, on undulating ground, again facing James across the river, centred around a few stone houses and a church which composed the little hamlet of Oldbridge. To the east lay some of William's forces. Protestants and

Catholics had been engaged in fire all afternoon, and there was a fierce artillery fight. There were few casualties. The Jacobite gunners were not very accurate, whilst William's men had managed to destroy some of the guns belonging to King James.

It was a hot afternoon and the gunners were soaked in sweat and exhausted after almost five hours of fighting. The six-foot iron barrels of the cannon were too hot to handle. The gun captains had held their firing power from the maximum of fifteen shots per hour to well under ten per hour. Some estimate that the opposing Jacobite battery fired an average of seven shots per hour per cannon. It was known that James's artillery was not up to scratch and he lacked a supply of ammunition and supplies for the gunners. However, the four main cannons represented a fraction of William's main artillery train. This included the massive 24-pounders, which were still at the rear of the lines.

There was a lot of gun smoke lying over the River Boyne, almost obscuring the vision of both armies. The last salvo of the day was fired by the Williamite guns.

The gunners loaded a pound and a half of powder into the long six-foot barrels. An assistant gunner stepped forward with a long wooden plough and rammed the powder down the barrel. A 6-pound iron shot was rammed into it. Each gunner placed a small pinch of powder in the hole. The gun captains crouched behind the gun in front of the Catholic parties, to ensure that the ammunition should reach its target, before stepping clear. The cannons were kept in place as they discharged themselves.

The final shots did not discourage the Jacobites, and William looked at the progress of the battle through his field glasses.

The Jacobite and Williamite guns fell silent for a while. The guns were secured for the night and the soldiers knew that there would be a lot of action the next day. The gunners could bathe their tired limbs in a stream that gurgled down a deep gorge near Oldbridge ford. They had their evening meal, and settled down for the night. They had gone to bed about ten o'clock in the evening of 30 June. They needed little encouragement to fall asleep, but they had been roused at about seven o'clock that morning to start the march to the banks of the Boyne. This was rousing the troops at an unearthly hour. They realised that the battle – the Battle of the Boyne – would take place on 1 July (12 July, new-style dating). Few seriously thought that the Battle of the Boyne would be of any significance. The generals gathered at William's headquarters in a former Cistercian abbey, two miles to the north-west of Oldbridge. Few soldiers in William's camp had little doubt who would be the victor – they outnumbered the demoralised Irish Army. William had about four times the number of artillery that James had; they were better fed, armed and supplied. Above all else, Protestants believed that God was on their side, as they cast their minds back to the Protestant victory at the Siege of Londonderry in 1689. No doubt James also thought that God would give him victory at Derry, and also make him victor at the Boyne. First of all the opposing forces had to decide where to pitch their tents and where to obtain straw and extra blankets. Each regimental waggon carried enough rations, which each soldier was entitled to before the start of hostilities. The straw and extra blankets were most important, for the nights were chilly despite the hot days of summer. Mists rose and lay close to the ground for several hours before the heat of the sun dispersed them.

Thirty-five thousand Williamite troops now lay encamped around the hillocks along the northern banks of the Boyne, from Tullyesker, just north of Drogheda and Townley Hall. There were many nationalities – Dutch, Danish, French, German, English and Scots settlers from many parts of Ireland, Swiss, Italian, Norwegian and Polish. All had pledged themselves to William and the League of Augsburg. The English saw in William a great liberator, for he had ousted the intolerant and Catholic James from the throne. In Ulster the common man saw in William the protector of Protestantism in the island of Ireland. Other nationalities saw William as a representative of the Grand Alliance formed to prevent Louis XIV of France from dominating Europe: Louis was supporting James to regain his throne.

The Jacobite army numbered 25,000 men, a great force of English, Irish, French, German and Dutch. But James was not so sure of victory as King William. Even the Earl of Tyrconnel, Dick Talbot, was very pessimistic about the situation. He had strongly advised James not to fight with the Williamites. He advised James to march westwards along the Boyne Valley, avoiding a confrontation. Condé also advised this course of action – he was commander of the French Division and Louis XIV's newly appointed adviser to James.

James decided to ignore all advice. If William did not make an attempt to stop James at the Boyne, Dublin would fall into the hands of the Catholics, so that most of Ireland would fall to James. James did not take into account that he might fall back into the wastelands of Connaught without supplies, and if this happened, it would only be a short time until the Catholics would be defeated. The Jacobite army might become demoralised by skirmishes with James, which were dealt with by King William. The soldiers were grumbling, for in the past weeks they had had to come close to James's forces with an advance from Dundalk. James marched to Ardee, and from here to the Boyne. James's own son, the Duke of Berwick and Major General Patrick Sarsfield had chastised him for not standing against the Williamites at the Moyry Pass, just north of Dundalk. From this position he might be able to hold up James's army for a while. Going against military advice James decided to make an attack upon William's forces. He wrote in his memoirs that if there was to be a battle, there was not a more favourable spot than the Boyne Valley. His main fear was that he would be driven into the Irish Sea. Tyrconnel and Lauzun had now prepared for battle. Lauzun said that a battle would not be avoided. He said, "I will, however, do all possible not to let it come to a decisive battle, for I said beforehand that I have some knowledge of the conquerors." He may have had in mind the rising of Londonderry in 1683.

The battle that took place on the Boyne on 12 July 1690 would decide the fate of the two royal houses of James Stuart and William Henry Nassau. The state of conflict in Ulster can be dated back to the accession of James II to the English throne on February 1685, at fifty-two years of age. James was not a man of great physical courage, sincerity, tenacity and industry. He had little understanding of his contemporaries and he would often misjudge situations and ancestry. Also, he lacked a sense of humour and diversity of mind. He was openly aggressive. Upon his succession in February 1685, he had pledged to protect the established Anglican Church. A few months after his accession there was a revolt in Scotland by Scots Protestants with a view to deposing him and releasing Scotland from the burden of a Catholic king. Monmouth's revolt was suppressed at the Battle of Sedgemoor and punished by the Bloody Assizes, with Judge Jeffreys presiding. Three hundred and fifity supporters for Monmouth were executed and 800 sold into slavery in the colonies. The suppression was ruthless and shocked even the people of England. John Churchill, who had made Sedgemoor a victory for James, said that marble was not harder than the King's heart.

The rebellion was used by James to establish a large standing army. But parliament chose to bypass them. James now lifted the position in Ireland under Catholic control. In 1682 he told parliament that, whether legal or not, they could not question the appointment of Catholics to the army. Both houses of parliament spoke out against this Catholic king. The situation started to worsen, and the assemblies were dismal. James did not check his impulsive behaviour and started to dismiss High Court judges and replace them with Catholics. Catholics were also appointed to the Privy Council.

It was obvious that James wanted to return England, Scotland and Wales to the Catholic faith and to establish an absolute monarchy modelled on that of Louis XIV of France. To accomplish this, James required Louis's money and soldiers. France had now emerged as the greatest European power, supplanting Spain and Austria. England had completed a triple alliance against her with Holland and Sweden. Charles II of England, who had headed the alliance, had proposed to Louis that the English parliament would help the French military. The Treaty of

Dover, a secret treaty, brought England into opposition with Holland. The treaty was considered with great alarm in England as a threat to the constitution of the Established Anglican Church. Europe trembled under the power of the Sun King and was also afraid of his religious bigotry. In 1686 the Edict of Nantes was passed by which Henry IV opposed Protestantism. He had decreed toleration and free exercise of their faith to his Protestant subjects. A hundred thousand French Protestants were forced to flee from France to Holland, Switzerland and England. Ireland was an obvious location for Protestants to set up linen manufacture by the French Huguenots, particularly around the Lisburn area of Ulster. Englishmen feared the army which James was now raising, and the placing of important offices with Catholics. Closed-down Catholic churches were now opened. Catholic religious folk – Carmelites, Benedictines and Franciscans – worshipped openly in the streets of London in their habits. The Jesuits set up a school in central London. Henry VIII and Elizabeth I had used their political influence to change the nation to Anglicanism, and James was now determined to use his power in favour of Roman Catholics.

The English Catholic gentry were in favour of King James's plans. Those who had opposed his religion were treated as hostile. In 1687 James tried to split the Protestant opposition by the Declaration of Indulgence, which annulled the penal laws against Nonconformists and Catholics. Popular Protestants like John Bunyan refused to accept the Indulgence.

England was on the brink of civil war in summer 1688. The Archbishop of Canterbury, William Sancroft, headed a delegation of seven Anglican bishops. James accused them of rebellion and ordered them to be tried for seditious libel. There were demonstrations in favour of their innocence and the court found them 'not guilty'. Joy was rampant throughout the kingdom – cannons roared and fireworks lit up the sky. Now a band of men wrote a letter to James's eldest daughter, Mary. Their proposal was that William of Orange should lead a rebellion against the Catholic James, himself landing in England. The gentlemen were Bishop Compton and the Lords Shrewsbury, Danby, Russell, Devonshire, Lumley and Henry Sidney. In England most people were of the opinion that Charles II should be succeeded by his daughter Mary. She was married to William, Prince of Orange. He had been called to the head of the Holland Republic after the fall of Louis XIV, whose army had invaded Holland in 1672.

William was a severe sufferer from asthma and therefore did not enjoy good health. He was only twenty-two years of age when he became Stadtholder and when he won back the province from the veteran general, the Prince de Condé. William had managed to form alliances with Protestant and Catholic countries to frustrate Louis XIV's ambitions. However, he had thrown in his lot with James II in order to secure the succession of his wife. Now William was confronted with a problem. James and Mary had a son born to James in 1688. He would become Prince of Wales. It was not good for confidence that Protestant England noted that his godfather was the papal nuncio, and that he should be brought up within the Roman Catholic Church. Rumour had it that the boy was not the son of James and Mary, but a trick to prevent his daughter's succession.

Upon receiving the letter from England, William agreed to take up the sword against Louis. On 5 November 1688 the Stadtholder landed at Torbay. But James was not worried, for he had an army of 40,000 men, and he expected Louis to launch an attack upon his old enemy, Holland, which would mean William's return to his native land. Louis now attacked Germany, which proved an unwise decision. The States-General of Holland gave their blessing to William's venture. James was now deserted on all sides, and even strong adherents, like John Churchill, went over to William. James was in one of his many dithers. His second daughter, Anne, let him join his rebels at Nottingham. James was broken in spirit, exclaiming that his own children were deserting him. James now tried to escape and leave London, but he was captured. A few days later he made a second attempt, this time with success, landing in France, where his wife and baby son had established themselves.

Influenced by the leaders of the revolution, William called a Convention Parliament. One section of the Tory Party suggested that James should remain, with William as regent. This movement was led by the Earl of Clarendon, Mary's uncle. Others felt that Mary should remain Queen in her own right. The matter rested with William, who would not be content to be an honorary consort. There was much debate; his proposal for the regency lost by only one vote: it was decided to make William and Mary joint monarchs on 13 February 1689. The Convention Parliament presented a Declaration of Rights to their king and queen, pointing out James's misgovernment and his determination that parliament should assert the ancient rights and liberties of English subjects. The King could exercise a dispensing power, to extract money or to maintain an army, without the consent of parliament. Subjects had now the right to petition and parliament should be the ultimate court of justice. William feared that the Whigs' policies would lead to a restoration of the Commonwealth Republic and this prompted him to recall parliament. It was recommended that an election should be held in which the Tories would be in a majority.

Louis XIV moved against Germany, but he was met with great resistance. The French Army had committed outrages, and had forced the Grand Alliance to be set up at Augsburg. The Alliance comprised both Protestant and Catholic members, in their determination to prevent the political and religious aspirations of the French king. Amongst the leaders was Pope Innocent XI, who had quarrelled with Louis. The Pope at first had condemned Louis, for he had revoked the Edict of Nantes, considering it a worthless sort of document. The French now bombarded Genoa; Louis marched on Rome in defence of the Pope, and caused Innocent XI to be a supporter of the Augsburg alliance. William was now head of state in England. Louis had learned that England had been an important pawn in his game of political and religious chess in Europe. If Louis could restore James, it would be a feather in the French cap. If he succeeded, it would create an ally against the Grand Alliance. In England peace prevailed, and not a sword had been lifted against James II. James was determined to hold on to his throne in a hostile England. A weak point had to be uncovered, and this weak point was Ireland.

The settlement since the Cromwellian wars had been confirmed by the restoration of the English monarchy. The problem in Ireland ceased to be one of Gaelic separatism, but one of land and religion. Cromwell had treated all Catholic landowners, whether they were Irish or old English colonists who had settled in Ireland at various times before 1600, the same. During the closing months of the Commonwealth, the old English colonisers, who had settled in Ireland, had declared for Charles II, together with most of the Presbyterians in Ulster in the first half of the 17th century. Those who flocked to Ireland during the Cromwellian Commonwealth were mainly Republicans and Protestant supporters. It was only after Charles II had agreed to support the Irish religions that the Protestants gave a blessing to the Stuart restoration in the person of King Charles himself. The old English Catholics had been deprived of their land under the Commonwealth. They looked forward to having their estates restored to them at the Restoration. The Catholics in Ireland supported the Stuarts in the belief that their lands would be restored. The Commonwealth had made its extreme land settlement in Ireland, and the new king had to disentangle the web. In fact Charles restored land to some of his supporters. The Commonwealth's colonisers remained secure. Charles had stated in 1660 that the Irish and old English landowners would have their estates returned; also that the Cromwellians should keep their lands. The 1st Duke of Ormonde (when Lord Lieutenant of Ireland) said that a new larger Ireland would have to be found to keep the promise. The land was a question that demoralised the twenty-five-year reign of Charles II. But on the whole it was to be a reign of compromise, peace and prosperity, with the Cromwellians owning much of Ulster, half Connaught and four-fifths of Leinster and Munster.

The position of the Catholic Church varied from toleration and semi-official recognition of the Reformation. Charles II was now entering the last days of his life. 'The Popish Plot' had caused hysteria in England. The Catholic clergy had to hide, and Catholic leaders, for example Archbishop Oliver Plunkett, were executed. Despite hostilities between

Ireland and England, Ireland thrived commercially. There were butter exports to Europe, salt beef to America, sheep-rearing, the Ulster-centred linen industry and fish exports. All these things helped in the growth of the colonists' activities. Irish workers were paid the sum that obtained in England and 80,000 Presbyterian Scots were recorded as having arrived in the year 1672.

The land settlement was perhaps the chief reason for the continuing rift between Ireland and England. James II had committed himself to the status quo in Ireland. Clarendon said that the King had no intention of altering the Acts of Settlement. The Irish and the old English let James II's Catholicism bind them to his imperialism. James was only playing politics. According to a Charles O'Kelly, the Irish looked forward in the hope that James would restore their position in the island.

Dick Talbot became leader of the old English Catholic faith. He had been created Earl of Tyrconnel in 1685 and he promptly set about filling important positions with Catholics and the Catholicisation of the army began. Tyrconnel was created Lord Deputy in January 1687. Satirical ballads were the order of the day and some of them were composed by the thirty-nine-year-old Whig politician, Thomas Wharton: one was centred around a couple of Irishmen upon the coming triumph of Roman Catholicism and the old landowners in Ireland. At first the ballad attracted little attention until it came to the attention of Henry Purcell, who set it to music. Within a short space of time it was sung all over the Kingdom of Ireland, England and Scotland. The song was called 'The Lilleburlero': 'Ho, by my soul it is a Talbot, Lilleburlero bullen a la'.

The old English and the Irish were now not pleased about the new move. Some thought that there might be freedom for the Irish race. It seemed for a while that there might be peace in Ulster and Ireland. Ireland was now firmly Jacobite, the Catholics getting back their estates from the Cromwellian colonists, while the native Irish landowners were still in a deprived state. Also they observed that their support varied. The landless Irish liked the idea of getting rid of the alien conqueror. Now had come the overthrow of James II in England, and this created a good deal of confusion in the kingdom. A black situation was raising its head. Rumours flowed amongst the colonisers that the Gaels, aided by the old English, would rebel, as they had done in 1641. The date of the insurrection was said to be 9 December, and this caused thousands to flee to England. "Every day ships left Ulster ports," wrote Dean William King of St Patrick's Dublin. Ulster declared its allegiance to William and Mary, and the gates of Londonderry had been closed against Catholic forces led by the Earl of Antrim. He was to investigate the reason that the citizens of Londonderry were making overtures to William.

Tyrconnel did his best to placate Protestant fears. The Archbishop of Dublin read a reasoned letter out to the people, courting friendship with those in Ireland and Ulster who were loyal to their Catholic king, James II. Tyrconnel kept up correspondence with William. Now Richard Hamilton, a well-known Catholic figure, was ready to receive the Duke of Ormonde, who had been sent to Ireland. He urged Tyrconnel to be steadfast in his support for King James. By March 1689, Tyrconnel was in firm control of Ireland with the exception of such flashpoints as Londonderry, Sligo and Enniskillen.

Louis XIV was now sure that Ireland was England's Achilles heel. It might be by way of Ireland that James might return to his throne in England. James now left France, and on 12 March he arrived at the port of Kinsale in County Cork. He was the first English monarch to set foot on Irish soil for three centuries. James brought with him an impressive following of soldiers, officers and arms. James returned to Dublin on Palm Sunday, 24 March, to great acclaim.

The Jacobites had underestimated the resolution of the colonists at Derry and Enniskillen to hold out in the face of Catholic forces. The Jacobites dithered over storming strongpoints. James summoned parliament to meet in May to put to right any misfortune his loyal subjects had been subjected to; he wanted reason, justice and good public order for his people. The ancient idea of a confederate parliament of an independent state sharing the monarchy with England seemed about to be realised. James did not like the idea. The Irish parliament introduced a bill to repeal Poyning's Law, so that the Irish parliament would be independent of England. But the bill was dropped under pressure from James, altering it in principle before it reached the English parliament, which had the right to legislate for Ireland. James did not entertain any independence from England and he had written that it undermined his authority. Parliament went ahead with its legislation. They passed an act that all religions were equal in the eyes of the law; and they ordered that each denomination should support its own priests and ministers. The main aim of the parliament was to repeal the Cromwellian land settlement. James's English advisers opposed this, and James threatened to dissolve parliament. The old English and the Gaels threatened to take no more part in advising James. The French advisers said that it would be in James's interest not to oppose the bill. James reluctantly gave his assent to the bill which decreed that the Acts of Settlement were invalid and that the 1641 landowners or their offspring were authorised to take up measures to recover their property. Outlaws that had emerged from the troubles were to receive a pardon.

The proceedings of the Irish parliament at Dublin had done considerable damage to James's reputation amongst his Gaelic subjects. James was determined to make Ireland a stepping stone to England, as Louis XIV had intended it to be. James did not want to make any concessions to the Gaels that would alienate him from English public opinion. Parliament had to be kept under English control. He did not want to repeal Poyning's Law. He attempted to block the repeal of the Acts of Settlement. James could not undo the English suppression of the Gaels. The old English conquerors wanted to lord it over the new English colonisers and both would still be masters of the native Irish. The majority gave their support to James, for the alternative was that the new English colonists would continue their dominance.

The Battle of the Boyne would not only bring an end to great dynasties, but would mean for the Irish another wave of colonisation – yet another land settlement. Confiscation would follow and the new colonisers might eventually outnumber the natives, which is what happened in America. The Irish race might disappear altogether.

Chapter 4

The Arrival of William

William arrived upon the scene on 14 June 1690. He had sailed from Hoylake, Cheshire at noon on 11 June with a fleet of six men-o'-war, commanded by an officer called Sir Cloudesley Shovell, Rear Admiral of the Blue. He had been knighted for his part in a sea battle off Bantry Bay during the previous year when the English fought an action against the French. Both sides had claimed victory. Earlier in the year, Shovell had raided many Jacobite ports in Ireland. There was an attack upon Dublin. He took out of Dublin a twenty-gun Jacobite frigate, reported with great glee in the *London Gazette* on 28 April. Under the protection of Sir Cloudesley's warships were six yachts and other vessels. On board the Royal Yacht *Mary* was William, and this was commanded by Sir Grenville Collins. Other notables were on board the *Henrieta*, commanded by Captain Sanderson.

William now knew that Ireland was the key in his ambition to hold on to the English throne and to confront Louis XIV. He thought that the commander-in-chief, the Duke of Schomberg lacked leadership qualities. The Ulster Protestants welcomed the new king and were holding out at Londonderry and Enniskillen against the besieging Jacobite forces. Now the forty-three-year-old Major General Percy Kirke was chosen to support the Protestants at Derry in May 1689. Kirke had arrived with four men-o'-war and twenty-six transports in mid-June, but it was not until 27 July, after 105 days, that the siege was raised. A few days later the Battle of Newtownbutler was fought and won by the Williamites, relieving the pressure on Enniskillen. Large tracts of Ulster were still in Jacobite hands. William had sent the Duke of Schomberg to bring matters to a conclusion.

Schomberg was born in Heidelberg in December 1615, the son of Hans Meinhard von Schönberg and Anne, daughter of the 5th Baron of Dudley. He had a long distinguished career in Louis XIV's army, but on the revocation of the Edict of Nantes he had joined the Elector of

Brandenburg's army, which then became part of the Grand Alliance. He had followed William to England and had joined a committee for Irish affairs, which decided who should fight in Ireland/Ulster. In March 1689 the House of Commons had raised an army of 20,000 men. They supplied it for a sixth-month period. It was hard to organise the army for the Commissary General, John Shales, had neglected matters and it was rumoured that he was sympathetic to Irish Jacobites. The forces were not up to standard and it was alleged that he had been bribed to make the purchase. Schomberg was officially appointed to the Irish command in mid-July and he sailed from Hoylake on 12 August with twelve regiments of foot, leaving the throne and the rest of the army to follow as soon as possible. Schomberg landed at Belfast Lough the following day where he was met by some of the colonists. They fell on their knees with tears in their eyes and thanked God for the arrival of the English, who had come for their deliverance. The soldiers said that never were people more welcome, and there was kissing of the soldiers for joy, according to the news-sheet *Great News from the Army*.

The Jacobites were in control of the Carrickfergus area, but they did not oppose the coming of William. The Jacobite regiments were present at Carrickfergus Castle. Major General Maxwell had a force of horses and dragoons in the Belfast area, which could have confronted William's forces. Schomberg expected an attack and declared that if the Catholics had any courage they would attack his forces by night, for they would not have a better opportunity. Maxwell had retreated and by early September had landed nearly 20,000 men, but other sources state that this number could have been as high as 30,000. The position was that there were nineteen foot regiments, including three Huguenot regiments, as well as two regiments of William's prize Dutch troops. There were six cavalry regiments and a dragoon regiment. In William's army there were the colonial-style troops at Londonderry and Enniskillen. Now Schomberg made a major attack upon Carrickfergus Castle, which was under the command of Colonel O'Neill and MacCarthy Mor. But the Jacobites sought terms. George Walker Story, a chaplain on William's side, blamed the colonists for ill-treating the Jacobites. They stripped women and children, forcing them to run the gauntlet. Schomberg rode with pistol in hand amongst the colonists in order to stop the Jacobites from being murdered.

Marshal Conrad von Rosen, King James's military adviser in the pay of France, estimated that the Jacobite army could put only six to seven thousand troops into the field, a third more being unarmed. Schomberg might now seize the advantage. With Ulster secure, he was free to march on Dublin, but the Jacobites did not like the idea. They said that it would be best to march his army across the River Shannon and entrench himself in Connaught until French reinforcements should arrive. James ignored

French advice. He was determined to win the day and march straight upon London, deposing the Prince of Orange. James set off from Drogheda with a small force of 2,000 guards and volunteers, reaching Dublin on 26 August. He ordered his son, Berwick, to conduct a delaying action in the region of Newry. Causeways, bridges and roads were broken up. Tyrconnel now went about organising a force that would defeat Schomberg.

On 2 September Schomberg left Belfast. He reached Newry on the 5th, but Berwick had completed his defences, and Schomberg's troops found themselves in difficulties. Potatoes were the staple ration, which also comprised the diet of the notables, wrote Story, potatoes being rationed in hard times. Barnet had laid waste the countryside and burnt Newry. He made an attempt to trouble Schomberg as he marched through the Moyry Pass. On 7 September Schomberg's forces camped in the marshy ground a mile north of Dundalk. There were storms and Schomberg's ships were delayed, and now rainfall played havoc with the Williamite forces. Schomberg was cautious; he liked elaborate planning and was unwilling to improvise. He made a sudden advance. This had given King James time to organise an army of 20,000 men to meet him.

By 20 September James had almost marched his army to Dundalk and Schomberg made ready for an attack. William wrote that he did not want to risk anything on his side. The Jacobite soldiers found Schomberg's action unacceptable. According to Avaux, Louis's ambassador to the Jacobite court, Schomberg would have attacked if he could have relied upon the Hugnenot regiments. There was less trouble about sickness, according to what a French soldier prisoner told him. The Huguenot soldiers were too unreliable. Many of them defected to the Jacobites. Schomberg was asked on several occasions, but he was for caution. William wrote again saying that Schomberg's life might be in danger. He pointed out that the Jacobites had twice the strength of William's army. The Protestants declared that William was informed of sickness amongst the troops, but some were well equipped for war and another substantial body were well disciplined and better nourished. Schomberg's only obstacle to believing that he would win the day was his usual caution, the weather and disorganisation in the Jacobite camp. William's men were borne down with dysentery and fevers and there was a great shortage of doctors and medicines. Many were sent to Belfast whilst others made ready for England, but the weather was bad during these winter crossings, so a great number died. Two thousand died in the camp near Dundalk; a further 2,762 died in the Belfast hospital, and 900 during the evacuation to England. Seven thousand Williamite soldiers had died, but now spring was coming. The British public were not kept informed of matters in Ireland – about the horrors of the campaign. The *London Gazette* wrote that the Williamite army was in good condition.

Winter was approaching, so the Jacobites returned to Ardee, where they soon became ill due to rainstorms, bad food and lack of sufficient medical supplies. Schomberg also retired and made Lisburn his headquarters for the winter. The Jacobites had achieved a moral victory and James was ready to fight William. A Jacobite captain, John Stevens, said that the army was ready to fight. He said that the army expressed a desire to face the enemy, but most of them were undisciplined and some went around naked. Most of Ulster was subjected to Schomberg, but as most of the native Irish had fled, they left behind the Protestants in control of towns and castles. The countryside had been devastated by the war. Schomberg was highly criticised in England. If he had been a good general, he might have delivered one outstanding blow as the Jacobites were fleeing from Dublin before the end of September. The Commons was now demanding a committee to examine urgent matters in relation to Ireland. William now decided to take command of the army himself, for he did not trust Schomberg. He did not consider that Schomberg was capable of a decisive victory. Only William would be able to make a good soldier out of him. On 4 June William had set out for Dublin with a large contingent. It was a rough crossing, so recorded the *Villare Hibernicum*. The wind was brave and the weather foggy, but it was not until Friday night of the 13th that they reached Ramsey Bay at the north end of the Isle of Man. On the 14th, a Saturday, the wind blew and William now arrived in the Bay of Belfast, from where he sailed into the harbour at Carrickfergus with his whole fleet. There were perhaps 700 ships in the lough, and they resembled a forest.

William came with the forty-one-year-old Dutchman, Hans William Bentinck, who tried to bring to his king's attention that the war should be brought to a conclusion as soon as possible. He was later to become the Earl of Portland, and he was attracted to the House of Orange, being a gentleman of the Prince's bedchamber. For many years his advice was listened to by William. There were also the notables, for example Butler, the young 2nd Duke of Ormonde. Ormonde voted not to depose James and make William regent, but he accepted the inevitable. He was created Knight of the Garter by William and took command of his English Guards regiments. Also there was Charles Montagu, 1st Duke of Manchester and captain of the yeomanry of King William's English Guards. There was Richard Lumley, an earl and a Catholic who had become a Protestant, who was one of the important personages wanting Prince William to take up the English throne. He was now commander of the 1st Troop of the English Horse Guards. Sidney was now forty-nine, and still an intrigue. Burnet said that his role in the revolution was an accident, in that he had been a confidant of William. Finally, the future Earl of Oxford, Robert Harley, was one of those who could provide places on King William's general staff.

The colonisers were impressed by the list of dignitaries: Important was Prince George of Denmark, the thirty-four-year-old brother of Christian V of Denmark and husband to James's daughter, Anne. George was the second son of Frederic III of Denmark. As a young man he had travelled widely in Europe and could boast of some hard training, and of seeing active service. There was, in 1674, an attempt to place him on the throne of Poland, which had failed because he did not like Roman Catholicism. On 28 July 1685 he married Anne and cast down his roots in England. He had a Lutheran upbringing and his father had started to change the constitution. King James seems to have had an affection for George. After George had supped with him they rode off to attack William, who had landed at Carrickfergus. James was sad and moaned that George had also deserted him. He ordered George's servants and baggage to be sent after him. He now became a naturalised English subject on April 1689, being made Baron Ockingham, Earl of Kendal and Duke of Cumberland, by William. King William was always close to George, a deserter. George liked battle too much and also favoured the Queen. His wife Anne succeeded to the throne. He was an otherwise intelligent man; he was mild of temper and free from vices, and was interested in solving the Irish problem.

King William, on his white horse, was met at Whitehouse by the Duke of Schomberg. This was the house of Sir William Franklin, husband of the Countess of Donegal. The house stood at Macedon Point, halfway between Carrickfergus and Belfast. William was very cold towards the Duke, an old man. Most of King William's followers met him at Whitehouse to be received by the new king. Amongst them was Count Schomberg, the Duke's third son, who had been appointed General of the Horse. The Count had visited England in the previous year, and had become a subject of Louis XIV, but he had thrown in his lot with the Grand Alliance as a general of the horse in the army of Frederick William, Elector of Berlin. Count Meinhard Schomberg had returned to Ireland on 6 June with an impressive artillery train to take up the new command. Also at Whitehouse was the Duke of Wurtemberg-Neustadt, who had been a soldier since he was sixteen. There were lots of other foreign names.

William now rode towards Belfast in Schomberg's coach, with the crowds cheering him – mostly colonisers and soldiers. Another coach, organised by the Duke, carried other dignitaries who had landed with their king. At the arrival at Belfast, people flocked forward to see 'King Billy'. Burnet, who was the Bishop-elect of Londonderry, and George Walker of the Siege of Londonderry fame, were both cheering for William. Walker had been Rector of Donaghmore, County Tyrone.

A speech from William was in order, but the Dutchman was bad at making speeches. Although he had spent many years trying to master

English, his accent was still defective. He refused to write English and lacked confidence when he spoke it. A newsletter was published called *A Full Account of King William's Royal Voyage*. William said that he had arrived for the good of the people of Ireland. Bonfires were lit as William reached Belfast, so that the whole town and countryside was ablaze.

The guns could be heard at Belfast, and there was a great shower of rain, which his subjects hoped was for their Protestant king. Captain Rowland Davies, the chaplain to Lord Cavendish's Regiment of Horse, upon hearing the news, headed for Belfast. There was a bonfire and fireworks as they passed the night in merrymaking. Jacobite agents witnessed the celebration, and they immediately set out for Dublin. It was reported that King William had only brought a small army to the field, since he did not wish to widen the political and religious rift between England and Ireland. He had also brought £25,000 along with several tons of halfpennies and farthings; orders were given to pay all the troops by 19 June. The Jacobites now expected the Williamite force to march south to confront them.

On Sunday 15 June, William attended a service in the parish church at Belfast High Street. Here he listened to a sermon admonishing Protestants in Ulster to take up arms against the papish James. William was a little surprised at the bigotry of his followers. Although William had been received into the Church of England in 1688, it had been for purely political reasons. William was brought up a strict Calvinist by Dr Cornelius Trigland. William was quite flexible about religious matters, especially when it came to expediency. He had a Mass celebrated daily at his chapel for political reasons. Following the service at Belfast he greeted several of his officers – in fact all of Lord Cavendish's Regiment were presented, including Captain Rowland Davies, who said that he had kissed William's hand.

Chapter 5

William Meant Business

Lieutenant General Douglas, a Scotsman, arrived at Belfast on Monday 16 June with a contingent of arms and ammunition for William's army. James wrote about this in his memoirs. The King said that he was the first Scotsman that had deserted to William's side, and he had earned the title of rebel. Douglas was faithful to the revolutionary party, and close to the King and all his followers. He took every opportunity to oppose the Jacobite party and interest.

It was a hot, close day that Monday when Bellingham arrived at Belfast. Percy Kirke introduced William to Bellingham later that day, and Bellingham pledged loyalty to the Calvinist monarch. He had kissed William's hand and promised to remember him. Bellingham now received a commission to serve on the General Staff as an aide-de-camp, for he knew the countryside.

The day was spent sorting out arms and ammunition from the ships. Captain Rowland Davies took himself up to the mountain to conduct a burial service for one of Captain Smith's troop. William was busy making a review of the artillery train, 'above forty pieces'. In fact his artillery consisted of upwards of some fifty pieces from field guns to siege guns. Artillery had fallen out of use in England quite recently and it did not give rise to any sort of trouble until the first half of the 17th century. Its development was mostly confined to Europe. The King of Sweden tried several new types of ammunition, especially in 1626, when he introduced a leather gun, which had copper tubing built into an external casing of leather. This gave it effectiveness and mobility on the battlefield, but it overheated after a number of shots, shooting 19-pound balls. After William had arrived in England his artillery made a great impression upon the English, who had not developed it because Cromwell had used it in one of his sieges.

King William's artillery numbered some thirty-six guns, demi-culverins with balls of 6–12 pounds. He had also several 24-pounders and some 19-pounders, together with howitzers or mortars, mainly for siege purposes. Backing up all this were the little 3-pound 'drakes'. The guns were fully charged and could have been dangerous to the user. Few could fire more than fifteen shots per hour. William was particular about the effectiveness of his weapons. The artillery was not significant in the campaign that was to follow, for both kings felt that it did not belong to the army. A technical force was expensive to keep in the field, and only a limited number of gunners were reserved as regular troops. Civilian labourers and drivers were brought into service, but they frequently deserted when things got rough. It was important to make gunners, fire-workers and drivers subject to the same discipline as other soldiers.

The main texts for understanding the artillery were Niccolo Tartaglia's works, mainly published in Venice in 1557, and Bourne's *The Arte of Shooting in Great Ordinance*, published in London in 1578. As far as gunners in the army were concerned, the standard text was Cyprian Lucar's work. A gunner had to be sober, always on the alert and to have good eyesight. He had to know how he could bring about the worst for the enemy.

King James's collection only amounted to some dozen or so cannon. The morale on William's side was good, for there were the great guns, some of which had to be drawn by eight pairs of horses or more. More than 1,000 horse were needed to draw the complete artillery train and its baggage.

On the same morning, 16 June, King James left Dublin for Ardee, the main camp of the Jacobites. An anonymous writer has given his account of the events that led up to the Battle of the Boyne. James marched out with his army, with 6,000 French foot, one regiment of which were Protestants and Dutch. They were well armed and well clad. Conrad von Zurlauben's Blue Regiment was the largest French contingent, consisting of two battalions of mainly German and Swiss troops, some of whom had been prisoners during the campaign against the Grand Alliance. Others had been taken from a captured ship and were given the choice of fighting for Louis or rotting. Most chose to fight for France, but they were always on the alert and desertion must have gone through their minds. The Walloon regiment and three more French regiments (which had landed at Cork on 12 March) marched out with James. They would replace Justin McCarthy's 5,387 men who had been sent to France to form the famous Irish Brigade.

James left Dublin with some support. He was in the charge of Luttrell, whom the Duke of Berwick described as an honest man. He was the eldest son of Thomas Luttrell and had married Catherine, daughter of Sir Thomas Newcomen, in whose regiment he was created lieutenant colonel in 1672. His father died in 1674, and he succeeded to the family estates in County Dublin. He had donated a regiment of dragoons for the Jacobite cause and as a result James made him Lord Lieutenant of Dublin and military governor of the city. His younger brother was Henry, a colonel of James's 6th Regiment of Horse. There was relief at the parting of the French troops, for they had abused their position as an occupying army. They offended Protestant citizens by displays of blatant bigotry. James was now in a difficult situation, for his attempts to gain Protestant support were destroyed by the behaviour of the French. The commander of the French Division, the Comte de Lauzun, had boxed the ears of Sir Simon Luttrell, and this was bad for overall morale. James now marched out of Dublin with a militia of 6,000 men, marching under the command of Colonel Denis MacGillicuddy.

Belfast people did not like the idea of leaving the town, and waited to greet William. The situation at Dublin was good for the Jacobites. Rumours had it that 100,000 people were about to rise up in England in an attempt to re-establish the Cromwellian Republic. The French fleet might cut England off from her position on the Continent. The French might be landing troops near Dublin. Sympathisers with King William at Dublin were confident that the 'person of quality' would support the Prince. The Duke of Schomberg was confident that the Jacobite army would have little chance of surviving, and there were many reasons why James was forced to leave Dublin. The main concern for the native Gaels was that they might be plundered and put to death and they were praying for the arrival of the Irish Army. But the Gaels were not prepared for a serious battle, only wishing that somehow William should be chased out of their country. King James had rejected the idea of burning Dublin as being too cruel and hitting below the belt. Lauzun, acting upon instructions from James's Minister of War, had urged their king not to make a full-scale battle with William, but to try to demoralise him over a period of time. The army wanted to withdraw from Dublin and burn the city before it fell to the Williamites. Lauzun wrote on 16 July that King James was not open to the idea.

James reached a position at Castletown Bellew, near Dundalk, where the main part of the army was encamped under command of the French lieutenant general of horse, Lery de Girardin. He was determined to fight for Dublin. The Duke of Tyrconnel, Dick Talbot, wrote to Queen Mary of Modena, stating that James's army would have to stand before Dublin. If Dublin should fall to William, all of Ireland would be demoralised and fall under a Protestant king. The morale in William's camp was good, and the army was well armed, so there were few desertions to James's side. Tyrconnel estimated that the Jacobite army consisted of twenty-six battalions of foot, seven of French and twenty-seven squadrons of horse and nearly as many dragoons. Altogether there were about 25,000 men. Reinforcements were arriving at Belfast, and Tyrconnel had to admit that the Irish were not as strong as William. King William sent abroad propaganda about James's forces: It was said that the Irish Army encamped made up about 36,000 men, all well clad and in good spirits. There were also 15,000 men more, remaining in the garrison. These claims would only enhance the possibility of a Williamite victory.

It is realistic to guess that the Jacobites could field 25,000 troops, for many of the regiments were not filled up to full quota, the majority of these regiments being under 200-strong and recruited that spring. The dragoons were little more than civilians in uniforms and indeed the majority had no uniforms at all. The only professional troops were the French contingent – the regiments of Zurlauben, Biron, Bouilly, Tirlon and Chémerault – but even their troops were far from ideal, and Irish troops had been requisitioned to fill up the gaps in the numbers. A few of the regiments had seen active service in Ulster – Sarsfield's Horse, Galmoy's Horse and Lord Antrim's Foot. The others had virtually no experience of weapons. Arms and ammunition supplies were scarce. The muskets that did work only had four pounds a piece. The French had landed supplies in March, which were substantial. Most of the foot soldiers were armed only with an iron-tipped shaft. The usual weapon in the Irish camp was the scythe. A Jacobite news-sheet was published explaining how gleamy the scythes were and this struck fear into the hearts of the Protestants. Not all soldiers could boast weapons; most had to rely upon a sharpened stick. As far as artillery was concerned, a total of a dozen cannon, mostly 6-pounders, one 18-pounder, and one 24-pounder were taken from Dublin. There were also a few mortars with high-trajectory shafts, which would be useless on the battlefield. There was little powder and shot to maintain action. There was a lack of tents and food and most of the Jacobite soldiers had to live off the land. James's army was far inferior to that of William's and morale was low, especially after the loss of Ulster.

One of the better equipped forces was that of Henry FitzJames, Lord Grand Prior of England. He was only seventeen, the son of James and his mistress, Arabella Churchill, and the brother of the Duke of Berwick. His forces were dressed in white breeches and jackets lined in red. Drivers were colourfully clad in blue and white uniforms. The grenadier company was in white and red, together with a badge displaying a burning city with the motto 'The Fruits of Rebellion'. It was in this regiment that the young English captain, John Stevens, was serving. According to the Earl of Clarendon, he was honest, sober and a scholar. His father was a page of the backstairs to the Queen Dowager. He was a Roman Catholic, but they were good and quiet people. Stevens had served in the army of Portugal, and when James was deposed he had been an excise collector. In 1689 he joined James in France and declared that he was on the rightful king's side. He was familiar with Ireland, with Drogheda and Limerick and had lived in Dublin for a while. Stevens was a man of letters, and before going into exile, with the victory of William, he had written various works as well as translations. He had begun a journal in 1689, which he always used up to the day of the Battle of Aughrim. At this point the narrative ends. There is no explanation as to the loss of the diary.

Castletown Bellew, near Dundalk, saw the moving of troops in the Grand Prince's Regiment into the area. The regiment was taking it easy until they were woken between 2 a.m. and 3 a.m. by drums beating to quarters. They were told to march troops through Tallanstown and County Louth. Now was put forward the grand plan for Ireland. Louth was quite a cultivated county, with large undulating fields. As the soldiers marched through Louth they remarked on the poverty-stricken nature of the inhabitants, as the result of rebellion. The enclosures had been broken down and the fields overgrown, for there were no herds of cattle to eat the grass. Stevens marched through Louth itself, which they said was a very poor inconsiderable village with no sign of its former glory – a phenomenon throughout the island. The Grand Prior now established his headquarters at Castletown Bellew, about a mile from Dundalk, in a mansion belonging to the Lord Lieutenant of County Louth, Lord James Bellow, who had been made a privy counsellor. It was an exhausting march and Stevens had some suggestions for his superiors.

James's army was now centred at Dundalk. Here James had confronted Schomberg last autumn. Tyrconnel's and Galmoy's troops arrived on 18 June, and there was now some hope in the Jacobite camp. James wanted to come to grips with William, but William was not to be rushed. He was up early on the morning of 17 June to review Lord Cavendish's Regiment of Horse in Belfast Park. He rode between all ranks and marched forward. William now pursued the policy of meeting the more impartial members of his army in person, to show that he wanted to share the same hardships and problems.

Chapter 6

The Excitement Grows

Another contingent arrived at Hoylake in the Wirral on 18 June and disembarked at Whitehouse, following in William's footsteps. A French trooper kept a diary of events and was impressed by Belfast, which he described as a large pretty town, situated on the Lagan and Belfast Lough. A long rise overlooked the town – what became known as the Cave Hill – a pleasant expanse. They were drenched by rain and clouds at the bottom. The town was teeming with William's soldiers, and the King wanted to consolidate his forces before the march on Dublin. The 7,000-strong soldiers were stationed at Counties Londonderry and Antrim. William ordered the camp commander, the Duke of Wurtemberg-Neustadt to start his march south, and the cavalry galloped forth from South Belfast. That day the Duke moved his men from Galgorm Castle near Ballymena to Lisburn. Ten days later the Danish troops joined forces at a point to the west of Armagh.

The mood of excitement had now spread to Dublin, but the military governor was not at all clear about his position. The Jacobites were so open as to tell their Protestant friends very lately that they would be glad to go into battle within the present month. The great number of Williamites at Belfast might cause social and political unrest. Security measures were now taken. A proclamation was posted. Protestants had of late come into Dublin, some of whom were armed with swords, pistols and other weapons, contrary to William's wishes. The date was 19 June, a Thursday. The proclamation ordered that all Belfast men bearing swords or bayonets were to be arrested. By now all suspected supporters of William had been arrested and many were imprisoned; the term Protestant was now identified with the Williamites. They were arrested with 200 others from Sir Thomas Wouthwell's party at Galway. They were taken to a church with the rest of the Newgate prisoners; prisoners of war were removed from Kilmainham to St John's Church. Many arrests were made over the next few days, and amongst those arrested on 24 June was the Anglican Bishop of Meath, Anthony Dopping. Also arrested was William King, Dean of St Patrick's Cathedral. King had been in gaol before. He was an active Williamite and had been appointed to help watch over the diocese of Dublin, but in 1689 the Williamite Bishop, Archbishop Francis March, left for the safety of London. James now decided that it was best to round up the Williamite forces at Dublin, after the defeat of his forces in Scotland. He was driven away from Londonderry and out of Newtownbutler. Dean King wrote that on 25 July he and many others were arrested and imprisoned. He was suspected again and wrote that he was again sent to prison with at least 3,000 Protestants and there he remained until William's victory at the Boyne water.

There was excitement in the Jacobite camp in the early hours of 19 June. The camp was roused at 3 a.m. by a general beat to arms, and about one or two hours later the entire force was standing in the river. They marched off a half a mile down the road to Newry. Stevens exclaimed that he had beat the alarm and that the enemy was just down the road from their position. The cavalry advanced, several parties being sent out. The horse and dragoons eventually returned to the camp, but the foot continued at arms until nine o'clock. That evening, William set out for Lisburn in order to dine with the Duke of Schomberg and to discuss the situation. William passed through Lambeg. Here he met a Huguenot, Rene Bulmer, who had settled in the area after the revocation of the Edict of Nantes. Bulmer asked if he could embrace William, who, on seeing Bulmer's pretty wife, with a twinkle in his eye said yes, and embraced her also. There was a rainstorm two miles down the road from Lisburn, and they took shelter under some trees. William stayed at the shelter until the rain had stopped, suffering from a severe headache. The locals granted William and his men refreshments. The owner of the house changed the name from Malon Grove to Orange Grove. When William reached Lisburn he ate with the Duke and the talk was about the battle situation. The Duke had already written to William that the most likely place for James to make a stand was at the River Boyne near Drogheda.

He had also mentioned that the easiest way to reach Dublin would be to cross at Navan further up the Boyne. He was supported by one Dan Golbornen, who on 31 May had written that James had arrived with his forces at the river and had fortified all places; and upon this river James and William would confront each other. William wanted immediate action and he inspected the troops encamped at Blaris Moor, and rode into Hillsborough with Prince Georg of Daamstadt, the Duke of Ormonde and Lieutenant General Douglas. Also Captain Rowland Davies, joining the forces at Lambeg, rode with William to Hillsborough. But now the numbers of forces at Belfast were supplemented with a further 2,500 horse. On Saturday, 2 June most of the time was spent in arming the camp at Hillsborough. Friday had been a quiet day for the Jacobite army; they rested from the troubles of the previous day. French regiments had reached the camp and Stevens had found time to note the names, colours and mottos of some of them. He estimated that there were at least 28,250 men in the camp. There were rumours that the Williamites were advancing. Stevens reported that 200 fighting men out of five regiments, forty from each, were sent to cover the Newry Pass and to observe and enemy's advances. On Saturday, 27 June William proceeded from Hillsborough where he reviewed the forces encamped there, a force of about 2,400 horse and dragoons. There were the colonial elements levied from the English and Scots settlers, mainly at Londonderry and Enniskillen under command of Gustavus Hamilton, the governor of Enniskillen.

The Enniskillen regiments that had a terrible reputation. They consisted of three regiments of horse and dragoons, under the command of Colonel William Wolseley, an Englishman who had arrived with Kirke, joining Schomberg at Dundalk the previous September. They surprised the ordinary soldiers of Schomberg's army. They were dressed in a poor fashion, they were half naked and carried pistols in their belts. The Enniskillen forces were without uniforms and even if they were supplied with them they preferred to fight in shirtsleeves. Nor were they disposed towards regular army discipline. Courage was their greatest asset and they did not like being given orders, but they were told that there would be no food if they acted as they pleased. This was in contrast to Schomberg's normally strict discipline, but he let them go as they pleased. The Enniskilleners were sure that they could conduct a series of raids on the Jacobite strongholds. They were fighting for the return of their land – their farms had been wrested from them at sword-point. Enniskillen was a small walled town of some eighty houses, situated on an island between Upper and Lower Lough Erne under the shadow of a castle. Enniskillen had been founded by the colonisers under James I's plantation scheme, and its position was of vital importance – a centre of settlers from the province of Connaught. It was a bulwark for defending the Erne Valley, with a link at Ballyshannon. Early in 1690 the settlers in the area declared for William and Mary. Talbot had sent Pierce Butler, Viscount Galmoy, together with a small force in order to capture it; he did little or nothing so he called it a day. He left behind him a reputation of dishonour. The Enniskilleners developed their talents for guerrilla warfare under Thomas Lloyd, a coloniser from Roscommon. Several attempts had been made to defeat them, but they managed to avoid a serious situation. William was impressed with his rough-riders.

Chapter 7

The Stench of Battle in the Air

James was urged to retreat by the Comte de Lauzun. He said that James was too far from Dublin and that William could easily cut him off. He declared that the arms of James were badly serviced and supplies were short. The only hope for James was to withdraw, burn Dublin and march his army back to western parts, avoiding any fight with William until he – James – was in a better position and until William's army was weakened by shortage of supplies and illness. James did not take Lauzun's advice; he had seen little active service and had only won the post because he was a husband of Louis XIV's cousin.

Lauzun had been a favourite of Louis XIV, and he had the cheek to ask Louis for the hand of the Princess. They had been in love for some years. They requested that the marriage should compete with royal events. Louis refused – instead he offered to make terms with Lauzun, and to make him a Marshal of France. He would also be created duke and governor of the province. He had been used to the promises, and the Princess managed to get Lauzun out of gaol. He escaped to England. He at last amended his relations with Louis and was given the command of a 6,000-strong French force. He was created James's military adviser. He had relied upon the military advice of the Marquis de la Hoguette.

James did not follow Lauzun and said to him that he was going to strip the countryside before William arrived. Scorched earth policy would weaken William before he reached Dublin. Lauzun had passed this incident on to the Minister of War, Louvois, who felt that James was being a little unrealistic. Battle now seemed inevitable.

The Jacobite troops had been sent out to observe the progress of the enemy. They rode back into camp on 2 June and were able to report that they had had some success with the first engagement of the campaign with the Williamites. They had some prisoners, one of which was Captain Farlow. It was early morning and Lieutenant Colonel Laurence Dempsey knew the stench of battle and death was in the air. There was also a troop of sixty horse and some infantry troops commanded by Lieutenant Colonel Fitzgerald of Lord Bellow's Foot Regiment, who had marched up the road towards Newry. They reached the Moyry Pass, where legend had it that the ancient Ulstermen beat the forces of the rest of Ireland. The Jacobites saw a party of Williamite foot and dragoons: they were about two or three hundred strong. Every night a guard of horse and dragoons were sent to the Moyry Pass. Their purpose was to take prisoners and to obtain information about William's position.

The Jacobites laid an ambush and opened fire on the Williamites as they rode past. According to the Jacobite author in *A Light to the Blind*, the Williamites had to retreat with a large number of dead. The Jacobites took prisoners, and another source also states that sixty were killed. It was regarded by another observer that the Williamite losses were sixteen men killed and some ten wounded and taken prisoner. Losses on the Jacobite side numbered amongst them Lieutenant Colonel Dempsey, who died of his wounds. He was from an old family with estates in King's and Queen's Counties. Captain Farlow was to prove a useful prisoner for the Jacobites. After questioning he admitted that William had an army of 50,000 men. *A Light to the Blind* said that 'This I am sure was an exaggeration for the King to fly before the enemy and leave him [William] in a country of plenty, of which the House of Orange stood in need, not having any sustenance but what was brought into Ireland from England, which by that time could not be much.' It was revealed that William was going to march his troops through the Moyry Pass towards Dundalk. Moyry was in a good position and a small force could defend it. James also had word that Lieutenant General Douglas was going to march on Dundalk via Armagh and Castleblayney, so that the Jacobite army would be outflanked. James said that the Williamite force at the Moyry Pass was in their strength overestimated. The King's eldest son, the Duke of Berwick, just nineteen, opposed James's plan and pointed out that the enemy was having a short march towards the right towards Armagh so they could have reached the plain south of Dundalk. James gave up Dundalk in order to retreat and take up a position on the right side of the Boyne.

Most of the Williamites felt that James might try to defend the Moyry Pass and Davies reported that two Scots ensigns, who had deserted that Sunday, 22 June, told William that this was the Jacobite plan. Sunday was a hot day, said Bellingham, who visited Sir Arthur Rawdon. He dined with Colonel Matthews, who had just taken over the command of the Royal Regiment of Dragoons. About 400 men had taken up arms. William was coming near – George Story's regiment was camping at Loughbrickland that afternoon, awaiting the King to review it. Accordingly he arrived with Prince George, the Duke of Schomberg and the Duke of Ormonde. The weather was still very dry and windy, which made for difficult marching. Story's concern was for the King's health, for the Nassau family were unhealthy, given to fevers. They died young or became ill during middle age. To this, William was no exception. William had a terrible cough and was of a weak disposition. His face was sullen and bloodless and lined with suffering and ceaseless pain. He could not handle a sword or warhorse until he was completely grown. He was asthmatic, but took good care of himself and was aware that he would have to suffer from a very early age. He ate simple foods, he drank little and went to bed early. It is thanks to his common sense that he was able to live.

William sent a messenger to Dundalk, warning the Jacobites that if they found his fields and houses burnt down, he would give no quarter to any man, either Irish or French. The messenger found great activity in the Jacobite camp. Later that night a force of 500 men were sent to discover the ways of the enemy. They were under the command of a Dutch major general. They did not return immediately and they reported that the Jacobites were moving out of Dundalk, heading for Ardee. The men were in good morale, but there were internal troubles in the Williamite camp. The centre of the disturbance was over pay. The War Commissioner and Paymaster of the Corps had not received any money from the Danish Chief Secretary of War. Nor could a loan be raised from William. It was reported that the troops were weary. A little money was found, but not enough to pay the entire amount to the soldiers. Some would not accept their pay and used mutinous language. The Duke of Wurtemberg-Neustadt reported that two soldiers had been arrested, two of whom were court-martialled and one shot. Five members of another cavalry regiment were arrested for mutiny. The mutiny was caused by the poor rates of pay in the forces. There was a court martial reported to the Duke and one man was shot. The followers of James were also plagued with mutiny and desertion. On 22 June a sergeant in the army deserted to the enemy and he was hanged at the head of the battalion. There were three others who were all Scotsmen and had served in Lord Dumbarton's Regiment. They had made good their escape from Flanders. Suspicions were everywhere and spies were rampant. On 23 June the main body of the Jacobite army prepared to march. The last to leave was the Grand Prior. The army started to move about midday, and they received food supplies – salt, meat and bread – in the stores. Disorderly soldiers raiding the stores were punished.

William now took to the field by raiding a few miles beyond Newry to ascertain the enemy position; he returned that evening. Story records the incident and mentions the great care he took of his troops. Later that day, Major General Percy Kirke communicated with William to report the return of Heer van Gravemoor's men. A trooper was ordered to climb to the top of the castle at Castletown Bellew. From here he saw a great dust arising towards Nock Bridge, which indicted that the enemy were matching towards Ardee. According to Story, William did not seem to be concerned. On the contrary, the Williamites were in excellent form. More deserters were brought into the Williamite camp and they said that the army numbered 20,000. William then had discovered the advance position, which made them withdraw. It was likely that caution would be the rule. The Irish quit their position in the face of William's men, burning their tents, but left the town standing. There was much confusion. The rear guards had panicked, having been told the true position. They performed several acts of indiscipline. On 24 June, James's army was falling back before William, and orders were given for the march upon Dublin.

Chapter 8

Arms and Armaments

The Duke of Schomberg was still nominally head of William's army. William made it clear from the start who would be in charge – the King himself. William had not discussed with the Duke what would be the best road to Dublin – here were the great forces of the Duke and William. The Duke's son had overall command of the cavalry and Count Solms-Braunfels was appointed in command of all the infantry regiments. King William planned to march in four divisions. The vanguard would be under the command of Lieutenant General James Douglas. The right wing of the army would be commanded by Major General Percy Kirke himself. The left wing would be under the joint command of the Count of Solms-Braunfels and Lord Oxford. The main body was now under command of the Duke of Schomberg and Heer van Gravemoor. Theoretically the army numbered 300 horse and some 34,500 foot. Many regiments and troops had been earmarked for garrison duties. When the army was reviewed at Finglas, near Dublin, a few days after the incident at the Boyne, it numbered nearly 35,000 men, including horse and foot.

William took great pride in the reputation of his Dutch troops. He boasted nine regiments of his Dutch horse, his own Home Guards, that numbered about 150 men. There was Bentinck's Regiment of 352 men, and the other European named forces with an average of 175 men each. There were also the highly effective Dutch dragoons, then some 611 men strong, commanded by Colonel Eppinger; and the Dutch infantry were also numerous. Solms-Braunfel's duty was to command all foot regiments and he had in charge William's famous Dutch Blue Guards. The guards consisted of three battalions, plus a number of cadets, numbering 2,000 men. There were five other Dutch regiments, with a muster strength of between 480 and 650 men each. There was also a regiment of Brandenburgers, which completed the Dutch contingent.

The next biggest regiment was Wurtemberg-Neustadt's Danish corps, consisting of three horse regiments (mostly Huguenots) but also eight foot regiments, also mostly Huguenots. They had a larger number of French Catholics, under the command of Colonels Cambron and Caillemote. William's officers had tried to reject all Catholics from the Crown forces as it was thought they might defect when they met their fellow Catholics on the field of battle. The French contingent also numbered two horse regiments commanded by Schomberg and his son.

The English and colonial forces made up only one third of the army, consisting of 13,313 men. William had two troops of Horse Guards, whose strength was 140 men each. There were also eight other regiments, including Colonel Wolseley's Enniskillen Horse and Colonel Matthews' Royal Regiment of Dragoons. Each had about 260 men with the exception of the Royals, which had 400 men. There were also twenty-three regiments, including the Enniskilleners, plus forces from Londonderry, Newtownbutler and Belfast. Although the army was well equipped, there was always the threat of action from the sea. The French fleet of Admiral the Comte de Tourville would cut off its supply line with England, so a quick victory was essential. James at first recommended a scorched earth policy, which might spell disaster for William. William might be forced to march through all of Ireland with few supplies and no way to live off the land. His army outnumbered the Jacobites. William was convinced about victory for his side. With its superior arms and discipline William thought that the sooner he engage James the quicker would be the victory.

The common weapon amongst William's forces was the musket – 6-inch-long barrels that weighed 11 pounds and 2 ounces. At a range of 300 yards it was, however, an ineffectual weapon, so fire had to be withheld until the enemy was a few yards away. It was a crude and cumbersome weapon, fired by a matchlock. This was triggered by a length of match and a cord boiled in vinegar to keep it slow-burning. It had to be ignited if action was near and kept alight. In rain and wind the weapon was of little use. To fire the musket the soldier had to take a charge of powder, and he was generally issued with a dozen ready-prepared charges before a battle. He rammed the charge down the musket, a heavy round ball and shot. The ball was likely to fall out of the musket in low firing positions. A short length of lit match was fixed into the barrel, and a pinch of gunpowder was placed as a primer in the spout, into which was stuffed the shot, and the trigger was pulled.

The memory of Cromwell's New Model Army of the English Civil War was still strong. A number of William's commanders could remember this sad event, for in Ireland the Gaels were driven westwards into Connaught, there to eke out a meagre living. The commanders had instilled into their foot regiments the art of volley fire under which the musket became an effective weapon. Soldiers had been trained by the colonists to load a fire in unison as a drum beat, copying the Swedish practice whereby three rows of soldiers fired – the first kneeling, the second stooping, and the rear standing. They were generally taught to stand in ranks where, after firing, the rank was immediately replaced by a second rank.

More efficient was the flintlock mechanism, used widely in handguns, but it was more expensive and therefore less common amongst the Williamite foot soldiers. However, only the Danish Army was in possession of these weapons, since flintlocks had replaced matchlocks during the Danish war with Sweden in 1675–9. Pikes were carried as well as muskets. This pike was usually a weapon of sixteen feet in length with a heavy iron head. It was to be used to combat cavalry charges, against which the foot were almost defenceless. At a cavalry charge the pikemen gathered in the first ranks, where they would try to withstand the first assault of the Jacobites. During closer fighting the foot soldier would try to confront his enemy with his musket rather than put faith in the cheap swords that were issued to the ordinary soldier. Very few of William's men carried the pike, and after the Civil War it was thought to be a redundant weapon. It had been abolished in the Danish camp by a decree in 1689. The bayonet was now introduced, which was a French weapon. It took three years before the English foot soldiers used the bayonet, so most of William's foot regiments were without defence from James's cavalry.

William's horse was of international composition and had a variety of tactics. It relied upon firing power rather than a straightforward charge. This practice, known as 'Dutch drill', saw the soldiers moving forward in ranks to fire, with pistols at the ready. They were close to the enemy and the cannons fired one by one. It was hard to relax in such a situation. Like the English, the Danes relied upon a quick charge into the midst of the Jacobites, using the sword. Cromwell's tactics in some quarters were remembered and the weight of a horse was used to dispel the enemy rather than by shooting or by the use of the sword. The Williamites were better armed, once again, than the Jacobites. There was no such thing as an army uniform, but each of William's regiments were issued with a uniform except the colonial ones. This transpired usually at the expense of the colonels of the regiments. The uniforms varied and were copied by the Jacobites, which during battles could be confusing. The Dutch Blue Guards could often be mistaken for a Jacobite regiment, Zurlauben's Blue Regiment, wearing a like uniform; and the white uniforms of Cambron's Huguenots could be mistaken for the white uniforms of the Grand Prior's Regiment, and also for the white of the French regiments. Distinctive badges were worn, so identifying each regiment.

William's army was comprised of well-trained troops, mainly veterans of European battles, led by professionals that would stand no nonsense. They were well armed, well clothed, and, on the eve of the Battle of the Boyne, well supplied. They outnumbered the Jacobites by 10,000 men, and had artillery support. James was unable to attend to his sick soldiers, who were gradually becoming demoralised. On the morning of Tuesday, 24 June the regiments assembled in their various quarters. A proclamation, signed by William, was read out at the head of each regiment before the orders were made to march. No officer or common soldier was allowed to pillage or to take away goods that belonged to the Gaels or to the Jacobites. The requisition of horses was prohibited; some of them were to be used by traders to provision the army. Outrages against the civilian population were condemned by earlier colonisers. Punishment for these offences would be death, as was the fate of deserters or those caught stealing or killing a brother officer.

Lieutenant General James Douglas's vanguard set out for Dundalk via Armagh and Castleblayney. Major General Percy Kirke, on the left wing under Schomberg, was to march to Dundalk followed on the right wing by Solms-Braunfels and Oxford. They would march through the Moyry Pass, then split up into various divisions. They would then be followed by the main body. The Duke of Schomberg laughed at the orders given to him by the twenty-nine-year-old George Clarke, William's Secretary of War in Ireland. Schomberg's plan was to split the army into two columns, one marching to the west through Belturbet in County Cavan to Kells and Trim. The other would march to Dundalk by the Armagh route. William did not consult Schomberg about orders in respect to these proposals. Clarke struck up a friendship with Schomberg, and the Duke had complained about King William's policies. Clarke, who had been proclaimed the true enemy of loyalty, said that he was generally perturbed about William's behaviour. Clarke had called Schomberg, 'an old Duke', but he wrote that he was a great friend. As Davies' regiment was marching towards Dundalk, they came across a deserter, who informed them that the Jacobites had an army of 43,000 men. They said that the Williamite Captain Farlow of Colonel Stewart's Regiment had been taken prisoner at a skirmish at the Moyry Pass, and now he had been lodged in Dublin Castle. The French trooper was confused about which day the army began to march, saying that on Tuesday, 23 June it arrived at Lisburn. Next day Bonnivert marched to Loughbrickland, where they joined up with other regiments. On their way to the rendezvous the army passed through Hillsborough. Here was a great house belonging to the King. From here they went to Dromore, near the bishop's house. This was the great stronghold of the Hillsborough Fort, which had been built in 1601–25 by Sir Antrim Hill to defend the pass at Kilwarlin on the main Dublin–Belfast road, for Sir Phelim O'Neill was up in arms. It was turned into a royal garrison in December 1660, and Hill was appointed Constable; he and his descendants would hold the castle indefinitely.

George Story was now serving amongst the other regiments that

Bonnivert joined at Loughbrickland. Story noted in his diary that they marched from Loughbrickland to Newry, where a deserter was caught and executed. He was from Henry Belasyse's Regiment, which had fought at Edgehill during the Civil War for the Royalists and which had supported King James in 1689. Sir Henry had now thrown in his lot with the Williamites. On the morning of 25 June, the Williamites entered Dundalk without opposition, and were cheered on. Wurtemberg-Neustadt said that the army was now assembled and that William would soon be entering Dublin.

Chapter 9

James Marches South

The Jacobites had completed their withdrawal from Dundalk on 24 June. They marched southwards by the town of Louth and Tallanstown towards Ardee, situated on the River Dee. (It was named after an ancient hero of mythology, Ferdia. In ancient times there was a four-day fight between Cuchulain and his friend Ferdia. He beat Ferdia and carried his body to the north bank of the River Boyne.) A general headquarters was set up for James in an old castle. He reached Ardee on Tuesday. Captain Stevens said that the army continued to stand in the same place and they had spent the last two days in exercising. The men were taught to fire, which they may not have been used to. The two days' training bore fruit for the raw recruits. Ammunition was scarce and guns were difficult to obtain. Few soldiers had fired arms during training, and most had to be content with wielding their pikes and scythes in an attempt to counter cavalry attacks.

On Tuesday 26 June, George Story's regiment marched on Dundalk. The Williamites heard great shouting at sea, which appeared to come from the French and British fleet, but it transpired that the fleet was friendly. Sir Cloudesley Shovell's fleet was at this time ascendant on the Irish Sea. He followed William's fleet south towards Dublin. Story set up camp a mile to the south-east, in an area which was used by the Duke of Schomberg in his confrontation with James at Dundalk the previous year. As the camp was in the process of construction, some soldiers from Lord Meath's colonial regiment stirred up a little bit of trouble not far from the roadway. William's men immediately set out in hot pursuit as the Jacobites fled towards the safety of nearby wooded mountains. They were overtaken, and in flight one of them was killed and another taken prisoner. The prisoner appeared to be a Frenchman and had deserted from Hillsborough about three weeks previously. Recaptured deserters were generally hung on the spot, and this deserter probably went to his death by this method.

That same day, Story's regiment entered Dundalk and Gideon Bonnivert's men were roused at 2 a.m. to march on Newry. Bonnivert recorded the scene of the countryside in his journal. On Friday, 27 June, Lord Cavendish's Horse marched from Newry along the Moyry Pass, where it was observed that the enemy might have stood in the way of advance for some time. Cavendish's Regiment reached Dundalk at 10 p.m., passing the Creggan River and Castletown Bellew with other regiments that were with them. They camped in two long lines, three miles in length.

At 6 a.m. Sir Thomas Bellow, with other regiments, arrived at Dundalk along with Major General Percy Kirke and the Count of Solms-Braunfels. Dundalk was deserted, although well fortified. Bellow's regiment was ordered to march through the town and camp further down the road. As they marched through the empty streets they observed the bodies of the Gaels that lay dead and unburied; others were barely alive.

The author of this information seems to have been in the same mind as Story, and they proceeded on the 27th to encamp on the plains of Dundalk, for much-needed rest. William's advance guard had reported that King James was now encamped at Ardee, not five miles away. Rowland Davies' regiment was only one of the many regiments that expected an immediate attack by the enemy. In a Danish journal it was said that 600 of the enemy intended to attack the advance guard. The Brandenburg Regiment sent out men to judge the situation and ascertain the position of James. They captured sixteen men and brought them back as prisoners to the quarters at Ardee. However, the dragoons were at the gates, but the enemy retreated.

Cavendish invited the King to supper and the conversation was pleasant. Attack was imminent and Cavendish's Horse had been put on the alert. He observed that at nine o'clock everyone was ready to attack and had a horse available; it was resolved to fall upon the enemy that night or in the early morning. Dutch dragoons had been dispatched and they fell upon the rear of the enemy, and some took prisoners and a little plunder. A report came in that the Jacobites had decamped and left Ardee. All were ordered to unsaddle. The encounter with the Dutch troops had taken place when a party of Colonel Eppinger's Dutch dragoons had made contact with some Jacobite horse. Major General Patrick Sarsfield had sent on Henry Luttrell's Horse to provide a rearguard for James's army and to hold out against William's position as best they could. Luttrell had nine troops of fifty-three men per troop to halt the advance, and this would help matters. They tried to harass the advancing troops and to interrupt communications in their camp. Henry was the younger brother of Simon and was the Military Governor of Dublin, and had spent some time in the French Army. It was said that he was clever and skilled in intrigue and war. He disliked Tyrconnel, which eventually made him change his allegiance to the Williamite cause.

He was Colonel of James's 6th Regiment of Horse, but he had not been very active in war. Eppinger's dragoons were sent and the Jacobite horse were sent towards Ardee without trying to engage. Story said that he was told by a general officer of Eppinger's dragoons that the Gaels had a small party of horse that knew the country. They kept themselves staying low in an undiscovered place. Now William ordered out 1,500 horse and dragoons to ride to Ardee to see if the Jacobites had broken camp. William was up early the next morning. With a small party of horse he followed behind to observe the situation for himself. He returned on the evening of 28 June, and Schomberg discovered that the Jacobite army had retreated to the historic town of Drogheda.

Captain Stevens, on the Jacobite side, observed that after staying two days at Ardee the place was no better than Dundalk, which had been plundered by their own men, leaving it almost desolate. Before the rebellion it had a good population, but with the Jacobite troubles most of the inhabitants fled from their homes and left the dead lying on the street. The enemy was advancing, and the Williamite advance guard was proceeding. The town of Ardee was now deserted. Fifteen men were selected from each squadron of Stevens' regiment to make up part of the brigade to march forward to relieve Ardee. Stevens was one of the soldiers chosen and he recalled that when they came into sight of the town the dust was rising like a cloud upon the highway beyond it. Dragoons were sent to follow them, bringing back two or three prisoners and a lot of heads of cattle, all this transpiring on 28 June. According to Bellingham it was a very hot day. Bread and beer were starting to run out as the Jacobites left nothing behind that night, thus benefiting William's army. At Ardee, said another Danish diarist, some 300 soldiers reported sick, but all were able to march, although with difficulty.

Deserters from the Jacobite camp started to opt for King William. They were the men from Zurlauben's Blue Regiment, for they were Germans who had been taken prisoner by the French Army a year ago in Brussels. The Germans were full of praise for the French, for they provided the French with pay and uniforms. They had not been short of anything else. They would not serve in the Williamite army, and they only wished for passes to travel to Germany. The French contingent of the Jacobite army, which arrived in Ireland in March, was well looked after, and Zurlauben seems to have been an enthusiastic commander. There was a skirmish in the Williamite camp on the afternoon of 28 June. A man and a woman were seized, caught trying to poison the water supplies. They were killed by the mob. Story says that the incident did not occur until the next day. He was confident that they were guilty and he says the incident happened on Sunday morning. The soldiers retreated and they accused the Irish men and women of trying to demoralise the

Williamite camp and to destroy the King and his army. The women were lynched by the soldiers and they cut the men to pieces. The Danish diarist said that two pounds of arsenic for poisoning the water were found by two spies, who were cut to pieces by the English.

The Jacobite army was now camped near Drogheda in a position where the River Boyne was near. James was aware of the nearest Williamite forces. Ammunition was measured out and orders were afoot to take down all tents and dispose of the baggage. The whole army now marched out without the beating of drums and stood on the alert all night, expecting the approach of the enemy. The main body of William's forces passed through Ardee, and the author of *Villare Hibernicum* wrote that the town had been plundered, leaving standing nothing but houses with bare walls. All that were left were the bedridden people. Four people had been murdered in cold blood. A Scots soldier and a woman were hanged.

Mullenause, the doctor, passed through Ardee that Sunday and he too looked upon the misery of the place. Story's regiment encamped in the cornfields by a small village. Ardee was situated on rich soil and had been a strongpoint, as witness the great towers, still existing. The Danish diarist records that at daybreak Lieutenant Karl Gustav von Gram was sent forward with an English colonel and 300 troopers to occupy the north side of the Boyne. The Jacobites had kept an all-night vigil, and had been given orders to cross to the south bank of the river. According to Stevens, about daybreak, with no enemy appearing, the army began to march in two columns: one through Drogheda, the other to the Boyne at Oldbridge. They encamped again in two lines in very good order on the south side of the river, two to three miles from Drogheda. The river ran along the whole front. The attempt to make good the passes against the enemy failed because they were too strong to be engaged in plain field battle. Von Gram's forces encountered about 100 Jacobite horse. Von Gram wanted to attack immediately, being superior in numbers. He succeeded in capturing two prisoners. He was somewhat taken aback when the English colonel said that he had no authority to make such a move.

Jean Payne de la Fouleresse, the Danish Ambassador, was in Ardee when he was informed that the enemy had taken up position along the Boyne. Would James now make a stand? Many Williamites believed that James would continue to retreat in good order. The Williamite army hoped that food supplies and drinking water would be obtained. The Irish Army had retreated and the English had taken Drogheda. James's design was that he should not unnecessarily engage the Williamites in conflict. The English came firmly along the banks of the Boyne, thus making the way open to Limerick. But the enemy was progressing towards Dublin and James was determined to defeat it; he thought that there might be a battle within ten days.

William paid a courtesy visit to the Duke of Wurtemberg-Neustadt, and reviewed his Danish troops. The main body of his army was now in three columns by Ardee. Story said that they had marched within sight of the sea, and could see their ships sailing towards Drogheda, which seemed to be a disaster for the Irish. In Cavendish's Regiment the confidence of the soldiers was not shared by all. Two men were hanged: one for deserting, the other for betraying some of his own men to the enemy. Story obtained more information when a soldier was hanged for deserting, and a boy for being a spy and a murderer. A sergeant of Lord Drogheda's colonial regiment was gathering wood at Tanderagee when a boy came up to him and said that if the sergeant went with him he could could obtain herbs for food. The boy, however, was leading the sergeant into a trap, and five or six Irishmen disarmed him, carrying him to a nearby castle.

The sergeant was taken into Dundalk the following day, but during the night he escaped, being wounded many times. The same boy had lured some dragoons into an ambush at Legacory. He had told them that if they followed him, he would show them where to obtain the finest horses. One soldier in Lord Drogheda's force, who had heard his sergeant's story and remembered seeing the boy, caught him making another ambush. The boy was seized, and he declared that he had been paid half a crown 'brass' for every one of the enemy he could take in ambush. Also, he observed as he went amongst the regiments, what condition they were in, and where they lay. He also confessed to killing a dragoon by stabbing him in the back while his father held him. Story was present when the boy made his confession. The boy spoke English and Irish very well. When the time came for him to be hanged he was very much afraid of it.

Another incident happened on the same day. A French soldier had become ill through drinking water, and thinking he was dying he grasped his rosary and started to pray that the army would be victorious at the Battle of the Boyne. William was now very much elated, and according to Story he observed, the countryside and said Ireland was worth fighting for. On Sunday evening he decided to take personal charge now that he wanted the army encamped. Story took some time for viewing the countryside. He had heard all sorts of tales and legends that had come out of Ireland. On Sunday, Captain Davies had delivered a sermon to his fellow-men. Not all officers in Cavendish's Horse felt that committed. There were more desertions, this time involving members of the aristocracy. Davies went to his regiment's headquarters. There he found Captain Cross, guarded by two troopers who did not allow him to speak to him.

Chapter 10

Ready for Battle

On Monday at 2 a.m., 30 June, according to George Story, the army moved off 'very early' in three columns towards the River Boyne, which was only eight miles away. An advance guard was sent to ascertain the enemy's defences. The Danish Ambassador reported that at daybreak on 30 June they again broke camp. William led the army in two columns, and placed himself at the head of the cavalry on the left wing. The countryside was dotted with small hills, and as the army descended a fine plain was discovered watered by the River Boyne. Official reports had said that the ambassador was making a mistake and that William's men maintained marching order in three columns.

The advance was led by Sir John Lanier since the order to march had been given. Lanier was a veteran who had lost an eye whilst serving in France. He was later knighted for his services. He became Governor of Jersey and Lieutenant Colonel of the Queen's Regiment of Horse. He switched his allegiance to William and had, as Lieutenant General, accepted the surrender of Edinburgh Castle on 12 June 1689. He had a bad reputation, not prone to leniency. He burnt a large part of the west side of Dundalk in February. However, he proved his military skills by the capture of Bellew Castle, where he acquired a large number of horses for William's forces. There was a rumour that most of the forces were Jacobite in sympathy. Maybe this is why William placed them in the front rather than in the rear of the soldiers.

William and his general staff, aware that the enemy might be to the rear, rode after Lanier's regiment. They caught up with him when the enemy was about two miles from Drogheda. The Duke of Schomberg, Prince Georg of Daamstadt, the Count of Solms-Braunfels, Heer van Gravemoor and Henry Sidney marched up the hill of Tullyallen together with William. The Williamite guards could view Drogheda and the Jacobite encampment, stretching for two miles in two lines to the west of the town, and to the south of the Boyne. Bellingham surveyed the site through field glasses, pointing out the main flashpoints to William. Bellingham said that he was sure that he was some time on the hill of Tullyallen. The Williamite generals were in good form. James, on the other hand, had been warned to avoid a battle as much as he could, but he had decided to stand and fight. The Comte de Lauzun and his French generals had objected, and Tyrconnel threw in his lot with those who erred on the side of caution. But only a week before that Tyrconnel had been in favour of standing and fighting William for Dublin. He said that if the Jacobite army was driven from Dublin, there would be little hope of holding the Jacobite position in Ireland. Now he supported Lauzun. He had written to Mary of Modena from Ardee a few days before. Tyrconnel now supported the idea of marching to the west of the country, but he said that he was not afraid of a battle. He was of the opinion that if James was defeated at the Boyne, then the Jacobites might be totally overthrown in Ireland, and the Calvinist William would lord it over the Gaels as their king.

James paid little attention to Lauzun and Tyrconnel, and their attitudes were endorsed by his younger generals, such as Berwick and Sarsfield. He had carefully chosen his ground, and many of the Irish soldiers were confident as they amassed at the River Boyne – for it was a sacred river, beloved of the gods.

It had taken its name from a young lass who had wedded Nuada of the Silver Hand, an Irish deity who was king of the mystical Tuatha de Danaan. He had fought against the Firbolg tribe of Lough Corrib in County Mayo. Here he had lost his hand. The physician had replaced it with a silver one so that his name became Nuada of the Silver Hand. His young wife was a water goddess. She was told that there was a secret well which no one could look at, but she ate an apple and peered into the depths of the secret well. The water rose up and chased after her, and she was drowned at Drogheda. The path of the water formed a river which was named after her – the Boyne.

The River Boyne runs eastwards into the Irish Sea, thirty miles north of Dublin, and is geographically in the north of Ireland. The first bridge to cross was at a maritime town, the Bridge of the Ford, which the colonisers renamed Drogheda. Only at Slane was there another bridge over the Boyne, nine miles along the valley to the west. The River Boyne used to be a tidal river and ships could approach the town at high tide, but their draughts were moderate. The Boyne remained tidal just past the hamlet of Oldbridge. Oldbridge was a collection of stone houses clustered around an old church, about three miles up the river from Drogheda. The Boyne ceased to be tidal where the River Mattock flowed into the bigger Boyne from the east, just opposite Oldbridge where there were the first rapids. Before Oldbridge, passing from Drogheda, the river widens to skirt round an island – the Yellow Island – with an area of sixteen acres, and the lesser island of Grove Island, with an area of five acres. At this point the Boyne flows towards the north-east. By Oldbridge it makes a sharp turn to the south-east, past the mouth of the Mattock on the east bank and Oldbridge on the west. The river curves round a great plain towards Slane, on which were ancient tumuli – Knowth, Newgrange and Dowth – the burial ground of the ancient kings of the region, the Tuatha de Danaan. There were many fords along the Boyne, which could be crossed at low tide. To the south of Oldbridge rose the hill of Donore, which commanded a great view to the south. There was a ruined building on the hilltop and an old chapel on the burial ground of the Synnot family. If James had been in the church at Donore during the conflict, as was afterwards conjectured, he may have had little comfort in the remaining hill, where stood a tabletop grave. The hill of Donore was steep on the western side but it was not so steep towards the Boyne and Oldbridge.

James had finished crossing the Boyne on Saturday evening, and cavalry troops were left on the northern bank to act as warning parties. They had crossed in two columns: one via Drogheda and the other reinforcement (numbering 1,300 men) to hold Drogheda. His headquarters was placed on level ground to the east of Oldbridge, at a distance from the Boyne, beyond reach of the artillery. James camped in two lines from Rathmullan to Oldbridge. Only 8-pounder field guns would protect them. The guns were placed in three batteries, one near the road on the western side just south of Oldbridge and almost opposite the Mattock and two batteries opposite Yellow Island. James was sure that the fords opposite Oldbridge would be the best place for William to try to cross. The position of the Jacobite army was a good one; William would have to attack. There were several narrow defiles which ran down to the water's edge, and behind them rose on the north bank Tullyallen and Townley Hall.

William, a born strategist, took a careful look at the position as he peered at the grey tents of James and his regiments flapping in the summer breeze. Heer van Gravemoor laughed and pointed to the Jacobites, but William estimated that James had a great number of men at Drogheda. To the south-west was the hill of Donore, beyond which many might be encamped. The Jacobites may not have been showing all their numbers, but he was determined to find out what their numbers were.

Small troops were marched towards Drogheda and to Oldbridge to ascertain the determination and strength of the enemy. The Danish Ambassador reported that, with the help of field glasses, it was discovered that the enemy had not suspected that they were being carefully watched by William. The 'boute-selle' was sounded and there was a little confusion in the camp. Two Williamite troops surprised a party of Jacobites crossing the Oldbridge ford, and they had been able to capture a horse and a barrel of ale. Dragoons entered a house near Drogheda and discovered 200 scythes stretched across the beam. A scythe was brought to William, so that he could observe what sort of weapons the enemy had. Again according to Story, William smiled and said it was a desperate weapon.

William's scouts reported that the enemy held strong at Drogheda, and any crossing of the Boyne would have to be made by force and probably with considerable loss of life. William now ordered that Captain Pownel of Colonel Levison's regiment of dragoons should march towards Slane, at which the only other bridge across the Boyne stood. Pownel was sent to find out if the bridge was defended and if a ford might be made there.

The Jacobites observed the vanguard of the army appear. According to Stevens, early in the morning, the enemy could be seen from the hilltops beyond the Boyne. The poor fled before them. They marched down and placed themselves along the side of the hills where they had set up headquarters. William instructed some of his men to the riverbanks opposite the little ford at Oldbridge. Gideon Bonnivert was amongst the soldiers and said that there they saw the enemy. He also wrote that they were so near them that they could hear them speak. It was an unusual move to make to lead his troops into such an open situation. The Jacobites did not let the opportunity slip. A Jacobite battery of 6-pounders opened up on William's troops, who, however, stood their ground under the bombardment, for they had not received an order to retreat. The Jacobites found about 200 shot, and four or five men dead. The Dutch seemed to have been the main casualties. A major in William's 3rd Troop of the Gaels was wounded in the arm. Bonnivert was angry that no order to return was given. He thought that it was not wise to expose so many good men to the slaughter without heed, for there was insufficient artillery. There was some logic in the madness, for William's troops still held firm in the face of the Jacobite shots and bombs. The troops were still in good morale and, according to Davies and Bonnivert, the casualties occurred in William's Dutch Guard, the veteran of many campaigns. William knew well how they would stand under fire. It is hard to judge the written accounts of the Battle of the Boyne, but it appears that William was undecided what to do.

Stevens was a Jacobite, and he recorded that the Williamites brought their artillery into action in the afternoon. They fired at the Williamites with cannon and mortars, but there was little damage done on either side. William's artillery did not start until 5 p.m., but Story, Bellingham and Wurtemberg-Neustadt observed that the Williamite forces had begun returning fire about 3 p.m. By this time all of William's forces had marched up and encamped around the hill of Tullyallen. A temporary headquarters was set up on the ruins of Mellifont Abbey. Now that a battle was inevitable, William instructed a battery of guns to be set up opposite

Yellow Island, just south of the road from Drogheda to Slane and past Townley Hall. The force consisted of 6-pounders and four howitzers. The howitxer was a short, squat gun developed for firing at the enemy at a steep angle. A large battery was also established on a hill beside a narrow defile that led past Tullyallen towards Oldbridge, which became known as King William's Glen.

Next came the 6-pound iron shot. The gunners stood ready, observing the enemy through a quadrant or carpenter's square. Having ascertained the main points of the sighting, orders were given to fire. The guns blasted and roared, recoiling on their wheels. No sooner were the cannons still, than the crews were once more loading them – ramming the ball and ignition device. According to Story, one of the shots smashed into a house in Oldbridge, killing a Jacobite officer who lay sick there. It was thought that the Williamite artillery dismounted some of the Jacobite guns and their batteries. King James was to arrive at the scene too late. Williamite propaganda said that James had his headquarters in the ruined church at Donore, and had remained there out of harm's way until he saw the fighting that was taking place at the ford at the river at Oldbridge. James's first headquarters were just across the river to the east of Oldbridge. Story continued his account and said that a shot from the guns killed a horseman that stood sentinel. Bellingham observed that the guns fired all afternoon and destroyed two Jacobite guns.

A little after three o'clock, William decided to ride to Oldbridge, which involved a ride down the banks of the Boyne against his generals' advice. He wanted to observe the situation himself. His men rode with William to opposite Grove Island, where some Jacobites were encamped. William and his men halted almost within a shot of Oldbridge. They could see the stone houses of the village. Muskets jutted out from the walls of the stone houses, which were filled with troops. Stretching along the banks of the Boyne were several entrenchments, some of which had not been completed. William moved a short distance to a place where a stream passes through King William's Glen, emptying into the Boyne. They did not care about the enemy, and the party sat down to a picnic. They had been mounted since early morning, so they were happy to have a rest. Food and drink were now eaten hungrily by William's men.

A group of high-ranking officers sat on the opposite bank, and a troop of forty Jacobite cavalry advanced down the hill and halted in a ploughed field opposite the picnickers. As these high-ranking officers indulged themselves, they were observed closely through field glasses. According to Strong, there were five gentlemen of the Irish Army whom he identified as Tyrconnel, Lauzun, Berwick, Sarsfield and John Parker. The Jacobites, it was said, watched the picnickers for half an hour.

At this point there was a deserter, but the man could not give them much information, except that the Jacobites numbered 20,000 men.

William sat on the grass for half an hour, and some Irish came along armed and ready to attack, for William was wounded by the Jacobite fire coming from two shots from a 6-pounder.

Amongst the first casualties was Prince Georg of Daamstadt's horse: the horse fell under him, being shot in the neck. The second shot was aimed at William. Although of not great impact, it would have killed the King had he not been shielded by his thick leather jacket. He remarked that the shot could not have come nearer. Thomas Coningsby straightaway applied his handkerchief to the wound – this information was learnt a week later. According to the official account of the campaign, William's wound was nearly the size of a man's hand. He lost about half a spoonful of blood. The Danish Ambassador, who was amongst the party, remarked that the King was mortally wounded. William retired to his carriage to have the wound dressed. He laughed at the doctor, who wanted to bleed him. He called for his own personal physician, who applied a plaster to the wound. William now remounted his horse and dismissed his staff, proclaiming that he would ride around the camp with the Duke of Schomberg, making himself a less open target.

A rumour was still circulating that William was dead or that he was dangerously wounded. But he was now seen with Schomberg and there were cries of "God Save the King!" that echoed through the Williamite camp. Shots were also heard in the Jacobite quarters, for King James had prepared a speech for his troops, exhorting them to fight well, and assuring them that he would also fight by their side and at their head. Both sides were ready for a bloody conflict and to show their mettle. A great cheer went up in the Jacobite camp, raised because they had heard news that King William had been killed. A report of his death was circulated in Dublin early that morning, and later reached Paris where William and Mary were burnt in effigy. An anonymous author said that Louis XIV's main rival was dead. William's close shave was the occasion for many tales which were to circulate after the Battle of the Boyne. A story was told that the Duke of Berwick had said that there were a number of officers with William in their midst. It was said that Berwick had returned to his fellow officers and, pointing at the Williamites, said that this was now a splendid moment to conclude the war; the Prince of Orange had to be attacked and destroyed. This would be a foolhardy attack, but Berwick is said to have responded immediately followed by his officers. He attacked and defeated the Williamites, but William was not amongst them. However, it is certain that no great attack between the forces could materialise that day. For the rest of the day the cannons roared across the field of the Boyne. At this point a Frenchman deserted to the Williamites. He ran through the River Boyne that afternoon in spite of being a target. As night drew on the cannons became silent.

Chapter 11

Victory in Sight

William called a council of war between eight and nine o'clock that evening at his headquarters at Mellifont Abbey, a 12th-century former Cistercian abbey, two miles north of Oldbridge. The abbey was founded by the Prince of Oriel, and many apostles went forth to further establish the word, amongst them Saint Bernard of Clairvaux. The abbey had been turned into a baronial residence, but now it was a ruin. The Williamites camped upon this holy ground, around its great grey walls.

Most of William's generals were cautious, but some of them had urged him to launch several regiments against the Jacobites that afternoon in a surprise attack. William dismissed the idea, pointing out with a little humour that he had a phobia about undertaking anything on a Monday. Many of William's generals had passed the afternoon, as William had done, riding along the Boyne to watch for weak spots. The conclusion was that the Jacobite army had chosen their position fairly well. According to Benedict, a crossing of the Boyne by the river fords, held by the Jacobites, was not only a dangerous task but an impossible one. The Boyne was deep and both parties realised this. On the Williamite side there was a morass, behind which was rising ground, high and steep, so William could ascertain the position in the Jacobite camp. Defences were hurriedly constructed at those parts of the river that were easily fordable. Stone walls and trenches had to be overcome; the stone walls and fences which bordered the field afforded great shelter for James's men.

If William succeeded in crossing the Boyne, the Jacobites would not be able to make a stand. The many rises of the land gave the Jacobites a great opportunity to make a fresh stand. Foot by foot, James chased the Williamite forces. William himself had observed that the stone houses at Oldbridge had been entrenched and loopholed. James placed infantry and dragoons, which would make it a great fight if any of William's troops tried to force the issue. The Jacobite side of the river commanded the northern banks, chiefly near Oldbridge. Between Drogheda and Slane there were no bridges and the river up to the Mattock, just east of Oldbridge, was tidal. High water at full moon was about 10.30 a.m., but at the quarter moon low water was also about that time. The river was fordable at low tide and most easily crossed during the spring. On 1 July the moon was five and a half days old, so the tides were not extreme. Low tide was about 10 a.m.

The Jacobites had not much firepower, despite their numbers, but they were determined to dispute the crossing. William had to place his forces against a point in the river where the Jacobites were least expecting a battle. Attack had to take place at a point in time before the area would be consolidated by James. Schomberg advised William that there were two options: He could mount a feint attack at Oldbridge, and at the same time he could march the greater part of his army to Drogheda, crossing the river there after a successful attack. Alternatively, he could march to Slane, repair the bridge which had been broken up by the Jacobites, and cross the river here as well as by a ford at Rosnaree. Schomberg favoured the latter crossing since Lord Iveagh and his Jacobites at Drogheda would cause William severe casualties, and slow down the Williamite crossing for long enough to allow the Jacobite army to counterattack.

William's Paymaster General supported Schomberg's plan to launch part of the army at Oldbridge as a feint and then send the bulk of his forces to cross the river at Slane in a flanking attack. The Paymaster General, Thomas Coningsby, was also the commander of the English foot. Henry Sidney was supporting the line of action taken by the English officers, such as the Earl of Scarborough, the Duke of Manchester, the Earl of Oxford and the veteran Major General Percy Kirke. They all supported Schomberg's plan. William's relations with Schomberg were strained; he blamed him for the previous year's failure. The fifty-four-year-old Heinrich, Count of Solms-Braunfels, whose arrogance was not liked by the troops, put forward the idea that the entire army should cross in the teeth of the enemy at Oldbridge. He turned to Schomberg and said that the army should not have to resort to subterfuge when the men were capable of crossing the river, putting paid to all those that opposed them. But Solms-Braunfels' arrogance went with his bravery, which sometimes bordered upon stupidity. This made the troops support Schomberg's and William's plan even more. William viewed the plan as bold and daring, and it was in keeping with his own beliefs, which were philosophical. William was an astute politician and decided upon compromise between the two plans. The feint would be made from Slane, while the main attack would be at Oldbridge. A division would be commanded by the Duke of Schomberg's son, Meinhard, who marched towards Slane and crossed the river ford there. Confusion arose about these orders because Lieutenant Gerneral James Douglas said that the original intention was for Schomberg to cross the Boyne at Slane. The bridge would be repaired. The crossing of the Boyne would therefore not be made at Rosnaree. Schomberg was of the opinion that the bridge might take time to repair. Captain Pownel of Levison's dragoons had claimed that the bridge had been destroyed. Gustavus Hamilton appointed four or five of his Enniskillen officers to act as guides to Count Schomberg's division. They would be shown where the ford was at Rosnaree. It appeared that Count Schomberg did not mistake the point at which he had to cross. The confusion may have arisen later, for Douglas was dispatched to make ready for battle on the morning of 1 July. He took reinforcement divisions to Slane and crossed by the broken bridge. Count Schomberg's division amounted to 40,000 horse, 300 foot and two dragoon regiments. They made the river crossing at Rosnaree at about eight o'clock. William was sure that James would think first that this was his only thrust. James's left flank faced Count Schomberg's troops from Oldbridge. At the time of low tide (around ten o'clock) William would make his planned attack on the village. Writing to King Christian at Denmark of the early hours of 1 July, he received word that the enemy was in a strong position and that William planned to attack at about ten o'clock on the ebb tide, when the river was not so deep.

The Danish Ambassador was Fouleresse, who understood that it was William's task to surround the Jacobite army in a pincer movement. Count Schomberg would swing around behind the Jacobites, placing himself between them and Duleek to the south. The main Williamite thrust would push the Jacobites into the Count's forces. He remarked later that he did not think the Count had an order to cut off James's retreat. It appears that a pincer movement was the best bet, and that William did not want to bother himself by making James II a prisoner. William wished to spare the feelings of Mary, his wife, and he was aware of the political dangers involved. Going against King James was hard upon him, for it would be a great trouble to himself and his Queen, if James should be either killed or taken prisoner. Some believe that it was these circumstances that made William take Schomberg's advice. Victory might be as great as that of Ulm or Sedan. William's personal dislike of Schomberg was perhaps set aside in moments of crisis.

Count Henry Nassau was to command the rearguard of the Williamites, together with Lord Auverquerque and Hans William Bentinck: in these two men William had great trust. The council of war broke up with the generals agreeing that green sprigs should be worn in order to identify the Williamite forces. Green sprigs were the usual mark of identification worn by both the Dutch and the Spanish in the Netherlands, so that under William the practice continued in Ireland. The watchword for the night was to be 'Westminster'. Written orders for the army had arrived, confirming the council of war's decisions, to be circulated to commanders that night. The Duke of Schomberg remarked that it was the first order of its kind to be ever sent to him. The division of Schomberg and William was widened considerably. Once the council of war had concluded its deliberations, William mounted his horse, still full of energy, and rode by torchlight around his encampment. He stopped now and again to inspire his men – William knew how to encourage his forces so that they would cheer him on. They threw their hats in the air to assure their king that they would follow him to Hell and back again.

At the Battle of Mons, twelve years previously, William had led his men into 'biblical hell'. On 10 August 1678, France agreed terms with Holland. William believed that he had been betrayed by the Dutch merchants, and four days were to pass before he attacked the French Army. The army was taken by surprise, in the knowledge that this would also please William. The French gathered around the Marshal Duke of Luxembourg, and at the day's end William was repulsed with the loss of several thousand men.

The fact remained that William had never been capable of effective leading in battle. However, he remained a good officer and he was able to instil confidence into his army. By riding around the camp at night, his men were in no doubt about his concern for them. The Williamites would forgive the cold temper of their Calvinist king.

Poor health reflected his habits of thought, silence, caution and reserve. His English was poor, which seemed at the moment unfriendly. His troops felt sorry for his delicate constitution, his frequent cough and his frequent attacks of asthma. His face was pale, bloodless and covered in lines. The Duke of Berwick wrote that he would not question William's daring as a great man.

James now held his own council on top of the rising ground towards Oldbridge, beyond range of William's cannon. Like William he had little talent as a general. He had shown great courage in battle, but like his son-in-law he was himself of a personality which demanded unquestioning obedience in his followers. James had a large number of experienced generals to help him in his planning. The Stuarts were a stubborn lot, and this was reflected in James's personality. James was fifty-six and still determined to win the day at the Boyne. He ignored the counsels of the Comte de Lauzun and Lord Tyrconnel. Lauzun was acting upon the order sent to him by the Marquis de Louvois, the French Minister of War. He wanted to have William concerned with the Irish problem, chasing James for as long as possible. Refugees that made their way to the Williamite camp reported that the French had been ordered by Louvois to take the defensive and not engage in battle. Story heard from these refugees that the plan was to fight a delaying action from Newry southwards to the River Boyne. His hope was that there might be a revolution in England and that France's army would be strong enough to intervene. Lauzun had greatly opposed James's decision to fight and had won Tyrconnel to his way of thinking. Lauzun's military experience was negligible and James understood his position about engaging William. His men were becoming demoralised. If he abandoned his position on the river he would thereby lose most of the province of Munster.

The Jacobite colonel, Charles O'Kelly of County Galway, referred to James's retreat from Dundalk to the Boyne and said that the Irish Army had not lost many men in action, but the soldiers had now become demoralised. They should respect their superiors, for Tyrconnel employed many men of his own. Tyrconnel was ageing, but he was useful to consult. He, however, could not command Colonel O'Kelly, who was not himself very enthusiastic about the Jacobite troops. O'Kelly was seventy-nine years of age, and had studied in Belgium and fought for the Royalists during the English Civil War. O'Kelly found himself stationed at Galway. He was a member in the Irish Parliament for Roscommon, and a member of James's Privy Council; and he had commanded a Jacobite regiment to safeguard Galway from Williamite attacks. His knowledge of the situation came from his son, Captain Denis O'Kelly, who was serving in Lord Galmoy's Regiment of Horse. O'Kelly died in 1695 and he did a little writing, producing a volume about the destruction of Ireland, in which he told the history of the war, but disguised all the names and places.

James wrote to Mary of Modena, his wife, twenty days later, saying that he was well aware that he was not responsible for making mistakes; but if attacks were to be made, there was not any situation other than the Boyne at which he could regain his throne. The danger was that William would drive him back into the Irish Sea.

The Comte de Lauzun said that it would be impossible to put up resistance at the Boyne. He had surveyed upstream as far as Slane and found the river fordable everywhere. His counterpart, the commander of the French cavalry, disagreed with Lauzun, but he later said that the site was a good one for battle. He was afraid that that night James might win the day. The Battle of the Boyne was to be fought on 1 July (12 July, new-style dating). James agreed and said that it was a totally good situation, and the best in Ireland. He entrenched himself there and waited for the enemy, but his army did not amount to more than 20,000 men. William's army numbered between 40,000 and 50,000. The Duke of Berwick was delighted in the decision to fight and he noted that the enemy was about 50,000 men. The Jacobites attempted sieging in order to stop the progress of the Prince of Orange or at least give him less advantage. The position at the Boyne was just the point he was looking for. In spite of all opposition, James was certain that he could beat William if they stayed and defended the Boyne. If they marched away and forsook Dublin, they would lose their reputation, and the people would cease to support them. He decided to remain at the post he was in, in the hope of enjoying a victory for the Catholic Crown.

James was determined about his stand at the Boyne – but it was a great risk with such uneven numbers. He felt that he should not abandon Dublin and all of Munster to retire behind the River Shannon in the province of Connaught. Connaught was in the west, rich in grain. James had a regular supply of food, but he could not subsist for long. His troops were impatient for conflict; most of them were new recruits and they would be discouraged by a retreat. But James had little confidence in them.

Colonel O'Kelly, although he realised the dangers of demoralising James, continued to retreat, but he supported Lauzun in that he thought the Jacobites should have come to grips with William, but only if they were forced to. There were plenty of those who did not agree with King James's position and who thought that he had not defended the Boyne crossing as well as he could. If James had entrenched himself, William hoped that conflict would be near. Now William hoped to confront James, but the Williamites noticed that the Boyne was loopholed and that an obstacle had been placed over the river. Also the fences of the field supplied adequate cover for his army. By this count more fences were not needed. William had the larger numbers and this must have demoralised James. On the evening of 30 June, James decided to forward his baggage south towards Duleek in readiness for a great battle. The soldiers were told to display white cockades in deference to their French allies.

James expected the main thrust of William's army to come from across the fords around the Oldbridge. His men had destroyed the bridge at Slane and Lord Iveagh at Drogheda guarded the only other bridge, thereby defending the flank of the army. Lieutenant General Richard Hamilton had pointed out to James the ford of the Boyne at Rosnaree. Neil O'Neill's dragoon regiment was posted at Slane Bridge on 29 June with orders to ascertain the position of the Williamites in case they marched upstream to try to ford at Rosnaree. James said O'Neill was not posted there until 30 June. He had been ordered to hold the Slane and Rosnaree crossing but with the prospect of a defeat. James was confident. One dragoon regiment was placed in this locality. James considered that any crossing on the Jacobite left flank would only be creating a diversion or a Williamite race for Dublin. Lauzun reported that on 30 June the Williamites were extending their right flank towards Slane. William started to move shortly after 6 a.m. Most of that evening was spent in heading for the Slane crossing. In the early hours of 1 July a council of war was called to swiftly decided the next move. It was decided to move the main Jacobite position to the left of the Williamite crossing in the direction of Slane and Rosnaree at daybreak.

Chapter 12

A Call to Arms

There was a general call to arms at two o'clock in the morning. Captain Rowland Davies, the chaplain of Lord Cavendish's Regiment of Horse, was roused from his sleep. The long roll sounded the general call to arms. It was extremely cold for a summer's night, even in Ireland. The days were hot and the nights cold. A heavy mist hung over the field of the Boyne. The mist made it difficult for the cavalry to mount their horses, but they were an orderly troop. Cavendish's Horse was one of the first to get into action. Each man held his horse's head, whilst the other cavalry regiments, dragoons and foot, stumbled about in the dark and the mist. The sun, rising at five o'clock, was obscured by the mist. Count Meinhard Schomberg gave the order to march at about five or six o'clock. This division of almost 800 horsemen marched through the woods in the direction of Slane, joining the main road from Drogheda to Slane. The mist was a blessing to Meinhard Schomberg, who had just celebrated his forty-ninth birthday with his father and fellow officers. Like his father, he enjoyed a drink – unlike William, who was austere. The Jacobites must have known that the Williamites were on the move. James recalled in his memoirs that the general beat was heard before the enemy's camp. The Jacobites could not see William's army as a result of the mist. Count Schomberg's position was that his forces constituted the main body of the Williamites, but he would not attack until he was ready to do so, so he was grateful for the mist.

Schomberg's division was made up of 4,000 men, horse and two dragoon regiments, two of which were Dutch dragoons. Behind them, puffing in the mist, arrived 3,000 foot under the command of the English Brigadier Trelawney, who had five small guns. The cavalry also consisted of Schomberg's own regiment. There was no other French cavalry in the area, and the French cavalry abandoned the French regiments of Count Schomberg's own command. The troops were woken at two o'clock in the morning and marched off at about five, although some of the regiments did not move off until six o'clock, with Bonnivert recording the events. They crossed the Mattock river and reached Monknewtown; and Schomberg was dispatched with a small body of horse, and sent it galloping along the two and a half miles to the town of Slane. The bridge had been destroyed. Schomberg decided to check matters for himself. Slane was a good position not to be ignored.

In the Middle Ages it had been a great town, and at the Hill of Slane, Saint Patrick had preached to the Gaels and their king, along with the Druids. An Augustine abbey had been founded at Slane in 1190, attracting scholars from all over Europe. It had later been founded as a Franciscan abbey in 1512.

Schomberg was not interested in history, but the abbey was a building that might be fortified. He did not want a hostile garrison to attack his rear. He sent cavalry troops to report back the position. Now they reached a small group of stone houses which lay on the south side of the Boyne at Rosnaree.

Schomberg's men marched across fields, through woods, across to Oldbridge and Newgrange, which contained the Palace of the Boyne, where the Gaels composed their sacred literature. Newgrange was surrounded with standing stones; they called for more than passing comment from the marching troops. There were royal tombs of pre-Celtic days. Bodies of warriors lay in their domed chambers. They were erected to the glory of the gods and a great god – Aonghasa or Angus. Angus was a young god, a beautiful youth, who adored flowers. There was a water god, who gave his name to this great river of Irish history. Some of the gods were able to make the sun stand still for many months. There was the god of the sea and also the god of love. Major lovers would search Ireland for a trip to the bottom of Paradise, and to take part in the god's activities. People would be turned into swans and they lived at the Boyne. The musicians sang about great peoples and kings.

However, there was little music to charm Count Schomberg's troops on the night of 30 June and on the morning of 1 July. It was nearly eight o'clock when the troops came into view of the ford at Rosnaree. The Boyne was shallow here and unaffected by tidal currents. Bonnivert had come down a very steep hill to find a shallow river at the bottom of it. They marched onto a very fine plain. Here there was a party of the enemy, with four or five pieces of artillery ready to receive them – but this did not demoralise the men.

The Count's aide-de-camp, writing on the following day, said that the division marched five miles to the ford, which was guarded by 1,200 horse. He had mistaken a Jacobite dragoon regiment for cavalry and instead of 1,200 men guarding the passage where Schomberg had 10,000 men, there were only 480 men of Sir Neil O'Neill's dragoons with the small field guns. William was informed that troops were guarding the ford at Rosnaree. O'Neill of Killeagh raised his own regiment at his own expense. He had been ordered to Slane by the Jacobite commander of the area, the French Marquis Lery de Girardin. However, O'Neill found that the bridge at the ford had been destroyed and that the river was quite impassible. His second in command was Henry O'Neill, and he had reasoned with him. He said that it was purposeless guarding the river at Slane when the Williamites were able to ford the river at Rosnaree. At eight o'clock, as the mist started to lift, the sun shone down on a hot summer's day – said to be one of the hottest of the year. Sir Neil O'Neill's men were confronted by the first Williamite attack by 10,000 seasoned troops. The Jacobites immediately brought up three field pieces and started to pour a steady stream of fire from the dismounted men towards Slane, where the ford was very narrow.

Schomberg's object was to draw O'Neill's fire and judge what opposition he would have to contend with. Schomberg had sent 100 of his loyalist grenadiers across the Boyne. O'Neill mounted his men and orderd the attack. The Count observed that the enemy were driven back two miles. The infantry were left to cross as best they could. The Jacobite position had been broken. O'Neill received a wound in the thigh and several of his officers had fallen. O'Neill bled profusely from the wound and was taken from the field. He died eight days later at Waterford. James had written in his memoirs that Sir Neil O'Neill's dragoons played their part well and disputed the passage by the enemy. There was much cannon-firing and an officer or two were wounded. James's sources were unreliable; O'Neill's dragoons left fifty of their men and fellow soldiers on the field before retreating.

Schomberg had crossed the first Williamite bridgehead across the River Boyne at 9.30 a.m. with little loss of life. One officer was badly wounded. St Felix sent a dispatch to William's general staff headquarters to let him know the situation. He had ridden hard, reaching William at the same time as Schomberg reached the south bank. William was delighted with the turn of events and ordered Lieutenant General Douglas to march after Count Schomberg with reinforcements for the cavalry at the bridge.

Once Marquis Lery de Girardin had heard of William's attack on O'Neill's position he sent messages from his immediate commander, the Comte de Lauzun, and said that the Williamites had crossed the Boyne below Slane. Lauzun now met William's troops and informed James that William's men were making their attack. James's left flank under Lauzun started to march towards Rosnaree, taking their most experienced troops. The French contingent was under the command of many notables; they brought with them six of the Jacobite 6-pounder field guns. James now feared that William would be in a position to take Dublin. James now ordered that the most essential part of the army should follow Lauzun, taking it for granted that the main body of the enemy would follow the right way. Oldbridge was now defended by two infantry regiments of the Earls of Clanricarde and Antrim. They were reinforced by a battery of field guns, one to the south of Oldbridge and the other opposite Yellow Island. Several regiments had already been withdrawn to face the threat on the left flank. De la Hoguette said that Oldbridge was held by only one battalion. This had been placed the previous evening, but they were now withdrawn early in the morning. De la Hoguette was misinformed about the number of troops there were at Oldbridge later that morning. James now withdrew a number of his troops when he heard about the attack at Rosnaree. He rode down to Oldbridge itself to talk with Tyrconnel about the number of men that were required to effectively drive William out of Ireland, and off the British throne.

Large numbers might have been necessary. Tyrconnel wanted James to have enough forces to defend Oldbridge in the event of an attack. He was left with seven infantry regiments, three cavalry regiments and two troops of King James's Horse Guards, numbering 5,500 men in all. They would soon have to compete with William's 15,000 troops. James had also withdrawn many troops which had been positioned behind the hill of Donore, commanded by Sir Charles Carney. These troops were made up of Nicholas Purcell's Regiment of Horse and Nicholas Brown's Foot Regiment. A further brigade of infantry, commanded by the veterans of Londonderry, was also moved from Oldbridge. No less than Major General John Wauchope was also moved from Oldbridge. Wauchope, according to Colonel O'Kelly, was Scots by birth, but was a devout Catholic, and he was instructed in Irish affairs. Reports came in that the regiment at Slane was in the hands of the enemy, and the order was given to join the Comte de Lauzun.

The mist had now gone and all movements by both armies could be seen. Lieutenant General Douglas's division was sent to the head of the forces that went off towards Monknewtown, which lay within the hills. Stevens wrote that they marched off towards Slane: "We on the other side of the Boyne marched forth, the river being between both for a considerable space, we marched under the enemy's cannon, which they played furiously without any intermission, but did little execution." The reinforcements marched on the south side of the river, to part of the old farm situated at Oldbridge. Now moving along the Boyne, and away from William's battalions, James skirted the 300-foot hill by the small number of deserted crofts, being removed to their left and joined them on the road to Duleek. At the crossroads, about a mile from Donore, where the road divided to Slane, the command was given to leave the roadway and try to climb the low hills in the west. It took two and a half hours for the main body of the Jacobite army to make its progress across the hills.

Meanwhile, King James and the major part of his cavalry and dragoons with Major Generals Patrick Sarsfield, Thomas Maxwell, John Hamilton and Alexander Rainer (The Marquis de Boisseleau) had joined Lauzun and the Marquis Lery de Girardin. The Jacobites had now entrenched themselves at a position straggling the Rosnaree and Duleek road, about one and three quarter miles from the Rosnaree ford. Lauzun had taken up a position south-east of a great bog, a mile north of the bog of Gillestown. Here flowed a rivulet, running south from the Boyne into the bog.

Schomberg now marched his forces into the centre of the bog. He was reinforced by Douglas's division, which commanded the river in three columns at Rosnaree and another ford a quarter of a mile towards Slane and at Slane itself. They did not think that they could make it through the bog. The Jacobites did not know of the bog either. Captain Rowland Davies said that he saw the enemy marching towards him and that they drew up on the side of the hill in two lines, with the Boyne on the right. Luckily James had positioned his men where there was a deep narrow gorge cut along from the river, along the path of the rivulet, into boggy ground. This presented a great obstacle for both forces. Lord Meath, who commanded his regiment in Schomberg's division, wrote later that there was panic in the bog and that the army was able to achieve a victory. The guns kept on firing, and the Catholics ran for it.

All this took several hours. The bridgehead at Rosnaree had been secured. From this time to the deployment of the Jacobite left wing – or rather, the main body – three or four hours had passed. The Jacobites were now waiting to force the issue, but James's infantry had not yet come up, for he was still struggling across the hills to Lauzun's position. But James as yet did not want to attack, for he was waiting for some troops that had not left Oldbridge. A red-faced aide-de-camp had galloped up to James's generals, waiting patiently for the arrival of the infantry. He told James that William had smashed his way across the ford at Drybridge a little further towards Drogheda. The Jacobites fled towards Duleek. The enemy had now forced the pass at Oldbridge, and the right wing was beaten.

Chapter 13

James vs William

The thick mist had disappeared around the Williamite camp by eight o'clock, and the sun had risen. There was a clear sky. Now the Williamite artillery started to send cannon against the Jacobite position at Oldbridge. The Secretary of War in Ireland observed that eight or nine cannon started to fire upon the horses, which stood on two sides of the road on the other side of the Boyne. Clarke was a keen observer, and his father, Sir William, had been Secretary at War to the Commonwealth, had served Charles II in the same way. He died of his wounds in the sea Battle of Harwich in June 1666. His son became an academic and did not like military activity. He went up to Oxford in 1679, obtaining several degrees. At length he became a Fellow of All Souls. In 1685 he became a Tory, and was elected to the House of Commons. He was famed for his scholarship. He had held office as Judge Advocate General, had been secretary to Prince Georg of Daamstadt and was now King William's Secretary of War. However, Clarke tended to be a bit of a sneaker. Many of William's followers in Ireland were to comment upon the Battle of the Boyne. Sir Robert Southwell, Secretary of State for Ireland, had found time to sit down to observe Schomberg crossing the river in the upper fords. The attack on Oldbridge might be ready to begin. The plan was that the Williamites were to encircle James's forces in a pincer movement. The moment of truth for both sides was near.

Bellingham had been up early and had been asked by Kirke to see if he could discover more information on the state of the Jacobite army. He included a youth who came to Drogheda that morning. He was carried to William, who was standing at the battery watching the cannon bomb the houses at Oldbridge. The youth could not assist William in his quest to understand the enemy. The author of *Villare Hibernicum* said that a Protestant deserter had swum across the river the previous night and he said that the enemy was 25,000 strong. William had rested well that night, and had risen early. By eight o'clock he had saddled up, making preparation for the battle. He was full of confidence, and sported his Star and Garter – this might make him an easy target. His wound troubled him, so he was unable to draw his sword. He had a protective breastplate, which also might make him stand out. A little after nine o'clock, Schomberg's aide-de-camp arrived with news of fighting at Rosnaree, and said that Douglas had been supported by reinforcements. William's cannon at Oldbridge was meant to demoralise the Jacobite infantry. It was now low tide on the River Boyne.

The northern slopes of Donore loomed up and here it was that Tyrconnel had reduced Ireland from a place of basket trade to the best paid rent in Christendom. He observed the gathering of information about the build-up of William's forces through field glasses. Tyrconnel had escaped from the massacre of Drogheda under Cromwell. Tyrconnel was now sixty. He had much military training, but he was not a genius. It would not take a military genius to understand the unease developing in both camps. If William was to make his main attack at Oldbridge, Tyrconnel was certain that he would not have sufficient troops to repulse William.

Talbot was descended from the Norman de Talbots. Henry II had granted them estates in 1174. They were a family that had been degenerate and had sunk to the level of the mere Irish. Richard was the youngest son of Sir William Talbot and Alison Netterville. His eldest brother had been one of the leaders of the Irish Confederate parliament of 1642. Richard had fought against O'Neill and the Confederates and later against parliament in the dubious Confederate-Royalist alliance. Another elder brother, Peter, was Catholic Archbishop of Dublin, and he had died in prison in 1680. Upon his death bed, Richard Talbot was in command of the army in Ireland. James had created him Earl of Tyrconnel. He now started to Catholicise the Irish state. He disbanded all Protestant militia. He had served James in England as an adviser, but returned in 1686 as Lord General, becoming Lord Deputy the following January. His ambition was clear – he wanted to return the estates to the old Irish in Ireland. He told Lord Clarendon, the viceroy in Ireland: "By God, my lords these acts of settlement have become damned things. We know all those acts a damned roguish contrivance." The role of the Acts of Settlement was now ready to be put to the test.

The ground sloped up behind Oldbridge. Tyrconnel had drawn up his own regiment of horse, 200 men with Colonel Sutherland's regiment and Colonel John Parker's regiment. There were in addition three cavalry regiments, and two troops of the King's Horse Guards commanded by the young Duke of Berwick. Under his command and commanding the first troop of the Horse Guards, some 200 troops were under the command of Viscount Dover. Lord Dover was first and foremost happy in his work, and he was an important Jacobite commander. He did not want to engage further in war.

On 19 June he had written to Major General Percy Kirke. He said that he might be surprised by a letter from him, and mentioned the revolution they had seen in their time; he said that nothing would be more wondered at. He instructed Kirke to put in a good word with the Duke of Schomberg, to obtain a place for Lady Dover and himself in the small vessel they would go in. A few servants were to stay at Ostend until Lady Dover wanted them returned. Talbot had served James well, and William doubted that James would flee from those that might have his head. The Irish had not in fact taken to James, and James's adviser, the Comte d'Avaux, had said to him that he was much estranged from the Irish. Dover had on several occasions expressed hostile words, but he had not received any word from William since his note to Kirke. Now he was involved in a battle.

Tyrconnel had two dragoon regiments – those of Lord Walter Dongan (a high-spirited young man, who was the son of the Earl of Limerick) and O'Brien, 3rd Viscount Clare. Both dragoon regiments were made up of eighty troops and fifty men making 400 men ready for action. Viscount Clare was a member of James's Privy Council. William had to find 1,500 men plus 800 dragoons. There were two regiments at Oldbridge, and Tyrconnel had five more regiments in reserve, making a total of 4,000 men.

Talbot's general staff felt the same unease. Lieutenant General Richard Hamilton, who Tyrconnel placed in command at Oldbridge, had seen his fear about the river fords being realised. He saw the attack but was it a real attack or merely a feint? Richard Hamilton was one of the most popular of James's generals, the fifth son of Sir George Hamilton, a younger son of Lord Abercorn and a cousin of Gustavus Hamilton, the governor of Enniskillen, who had defended it against the Jacobites. Even now he was waiting to lead the Enniskilleners across the Oldbridge ford. Richard Hamilton had been admired because he 'zealously protected the Protestants during his campaign in Ulster the previous year'.

Lieutenant General of Horse, Dominick Sheldon, also shared Tyrconnel's fears; he was head of James's cavalry. According to Kelly he was an Englishman of the Roman Catholic faith, and was brought to Ireland on the accession of James II by Tyrconnel, who made him a captain of a company of men-at-arms. Brigadier William Dorrington was another member of the general staff of officers. He was in command of the Royal Regiment of Foot. At full strength the contingent was compared to twenty-two companies of ninety men per company. All were well clad and well armed in red linen with blue. The Brigadier's regiment flew the royal colours of England, Saint George's Cross and the arms of the four kingdoms. The Royal Regiment of Foot was one of Tyrconnel's five reserve infantry regiments. Amongst the troop was a regiment of raw recruits.

The inhabitants of Oldbridge had fled to Drogheda, and it was here that the soldiers of the infantry regiments of the Earls of Clanricarde and Antrim sheltered themselves as best they could from the Williamite infantry. Large holes had been blown in the walls of the houses. Part of the church was damaged by the 6-pounder cannonballs and the heavy missiles from the howitzers. Alexander MacDonnell was not a stranger to this form of battle. He had started his military career as the commander of a regiment raised to safeguard the Irish Confederacy in 1642. From 1649–51 he had fought in the Cromwellian Wars under the leadership of the military bishop Emer MacMohan. He was at length forced to surrender, and he was allowed to take his men to France to serve in the French Army. His lands were confiscated and his elder brother, Randal, died in 1683. There was hope of restitution of his estates; he had raised a regiment for the Jacobites and had made an attempt to lay siege to Londonderry, one of the factors that started the great siege of that city. Lord Antrim had 650 men fitted out in winter jackets and knee breeches lined with red. The French made it to Oldbridge across a green field. Crosses were held high. In the centre was a harp mounted by a crown engraved with the motto 'By This Sign Win'.

There was a great commotion round Tyrconnel and he could follow the movements of William's troop across the Boyne, and the noise of sticks upon the skin of the drums. They saw the Williamites draw close to the banks of the ford. Tyrconnel now ordered Brigadier Dorrington into Oldbridge with the Royal Regiment to support Clanricarde and Antrim. He also ordered the rest of the infantry to take up positions along the south bank of the Boyne to the east of Oldbridge. The attack on Oldbridge started about 11 a.m. Others state that the attack started about fifteen minutes after ten o'clock. The Danish Ambassador supported this view. William had received word of Count Schomberg's successful crossing. The ford of Oldbridge was attacked by the foot soldiers so that the body of the Williamites could cross.

The first regiment to attack the Jacobites was the Dutch Blue Guards, arranged in three battalions of William's corps d'elite. The first honours of the Battle of the Boyne had gone to the Count of Solms-Braunfels. These same battalions had marched up the Mall in London, colours flying, drums beating, matches lighted, in order to occupy Whitehall for William. He was easy in his saddle when he rode up the Mall, and he gave the order for the colours to be raised. The drums struck up a march and the Dutch were clad in dark-blue jackets and knee breeches.

They began to march towards the Boyne. The English in William's army were annoyed; this they were unable to conceal. They agreed that the Count was a fit leader, brave to the last. However, his behaviour was rude and for no reason, and this made him one of the most detested of William's soldiers.

The drummers played 'Lilliburlero', and as they crossed the Boyne the jaunty strain of the music must have tormented the Jacobites. The Guards reached the river's edge, and Solms-Braunfels and his staff drew their horses to the side as if on a parade ground. The pipes and drums did not miss a note. The Dutch beat a march until they reached the river's side, and then the drum called. They entered the Boyne eight abreast. The crossing was attempted a few yards to the west of Grove Island. The Dutch went in up to their waists, carrying their muskets above their heads. The Danish Ambassador wrote to King Christian V that the regiments of the Dutch Guards were the first to cross. The Jacobites occupied a village on the bank, where there were colourful gardens. The Dutch Guards were 1,931 strong, almost the same as the Jacobite troops at Oldbridge. James's men waited until the Dutch were halfway across. According to Strong a whole peal of shots burst forth. The Jacobite infantry occupied high ground. The first casualty was a lieutenant of the Dutch grenadier company who was a prime target, sporting his uniform of piebald yellow and red, with his fur-lined cap. The lieutenant had been trying to form up men, crouching down, so that the Dutch could fire over his head. Setting the Dutch grenadier companies against the Jacobites was a strategic move. Each grenadier carried three grenades, each weighing three pounds, in his pouch. They were able to light the fuses and throw them into the enemy ranks at close quarters. This caused confusion in the enemy ranks.

The Dutch soldiers started to struggle on the south bank. Their numbers were great in the Boyne where they forded. Major Arthur Ashton, of the Jacobite Royal Regiment of Foot, led his troops to the water's edge. An officer of the Dutch Guards was killed by the lance of a Jacobite soldier. The Jacobite resistance to the Dutch was strong and the fighting was such that the soldiers said they had not seen such conflict. The Dutch now managed to push the Jacobites away from the river and back to Oldbridge. The houses and the walls still remained. The Danish Ambassador heard the news and wrote to King Christian V the next day that the Dutch rushed to the attack with great impetus, so that they were able to maintain their ground.

With a loss of 150 men, the Dutch had driven the Jacobites back. They continued their assault until the Jacobite regiment had been beaten. After this they were able to form up with military precision to await reinforcement. William decided to wait on the regiments under Gustavus Hamilton, who had been in charge at Enniskillen, and also the contingents from Londonderry and Newtownbutler. These were meant to march across the Boyne after the Dutch Guards. The two Huguenot regiments were to cross over to Grove Island, together with the English contingents of foot under Colonel Sir John Hammer and Colonel St John. They would be followed by the 625 men of the Dutch foot regiment of Count Henry Nassau, who had a joint command. He had persuaded William, his cousin, to use him in the forward troops. Nassau was forty-nine and cut a dashing figure. He carried a gilt sword, gold inlaid pistols and a pair of horse buckles that the Dutch States-General had presented him with after he had saved William's life at the Battle of Mons on 13 August 1678. He was the third son of Louis, Count Nassau, illegitimate son of Maurice, Prince of Orange, the great uncle of William. William rewarded him for his services and made him Master of the Horse, and parliament had bestowed upon him his English naturalisation in 1689.

Tyrconnel saw the troops moving towards their crossing point; he was now intent upon sending in the cavalry to force William back across the Boyne. Tyrconnel ordered Berwick to rally his troops of Horse Guards with Parker in support. The Dutch were now set up in lines before Oldbridge. Richard Hamilton was to form up first, and together with Antrim's men they would protect his flank from the Dutch. The Williamites were now crossing over at Grove Island. The Jacobites swung round the hill on Donore, confronting the Dutch Guards halted before Oldbridge. An observer stated that there was a great number of men and horses of the enemy. Three squadrons of James's bodyguard, which appeared to be very determined, rushed sword in hand upon the Williamites.

Not alarmed, the Dutch Blue Guards formed a square to combat the cavalry of nearly 1,000 men and horses led by James II's son, Berwick. William was on the opposite side of the Boyne and was viewing the start of the battle through field glasses, and he was not pleased with what he saw. George Clarke, his Secretary of War, said that the King was apprehensive, for there was no hiding place for any horse to support them. It was said that William cried out, "My poor Guards!"

Chapter 14

The French and the Dutch

The Duke of Berwick, from a very early age, was trained in the arts of war. He was the illegitimate son of James II and Arabella Churchill, and he had, by the age of nineteen, acquired a reputation as a soldier. Also, John Churchill, Earl of Marlborough, was soon to be made a Duke. Berwick had led the Duke of Lorraine's army against the Turks and in Hungary he served under Lieutenant General Taaffe, who had a brother, Francis, the 3rd Earl of Carlingford, now serving under him. Berwick would celebrate his twentieth birthday as the youngest cavalry officer of the day. He had a brother aged seventeen, who now saw action at Rosnaree. Some Williamites fled to France where they were educated as Catholics. They studied under James, and were very enthusiastic about his cause.

The Jacobite's charge against the Dutch was like water against a stone. Pikes were used – the main method of repulsing cavalry by infantry. The Dutch were the few Williamites that were so well equipped. The toll amongst the Jacobites was great and Lord Carlingford was one of those who met their deaths. The Dutch still held their squares as the Jacobites went away. Lieutenant General Dominick Sheldon urged his men forward and rallied them into a second charge. Again the Jacobites confronted the Williamites but again they were beaten off with great losses. Sheldon had his horse killed under him and Colonel Sutherland received a severe wound. William was greatly pleased by the actions of the Dutch troops. George Clarke reported that when he saw them stand their ground and fire by platoons, so that the horses were forced to run away in great disorder, he breathed a sign of relief. The Danish Ambassador was standing near William. He too observed the action, and said of the Dutch regiment that it defended itself bravely, so that the Irish had been forced to return with great loss. The Dutch remained masters of the situation.

The eighty-four-year-old Duke of Schomberg was riding about the field, rallying his men and looking for weaknesses that might be to James's advantage. The Duke had not yet crossed the Boyne. It was about eleven o'clock. William decided to make another bridgehead further down the Boyne under the German lieutenant general, the Duke of Wurtemberg-Neustadt. They planned to cross over at the extreme east of Yellow Island, about a mile from Oldbridge, getting ready for a flanking attack. The Danish foot and cavalry would be reinforced by Colonel John Cutt's Dutch infantry and by a French division made up of five foot battalions and six squadron of horse. The division was ordered to the attack by the Duke. Orders were given that everyone should be ready to march, and that the musketeers should strike their tents.

Richard Hamilton had led his troops of foot against the Huguenot regiments (not yet knowing the state of Sheldon's cavalry). The Earl of Antrim's foot, on his left flank, fired against Count Nassau's Regiment. Hamilton's infantry was made up of raw recruits – those that had joined in the spring but were poorly trained and poorly armed. Hamilton led them down the riverbank where they saw the regiments of Nassau. As Hamilton, together with other officers, was crossing the River Boyne, his men broke and fled, leaving Hamilton in midstream, waving his sword and shouting at them to stand firm and fight. It was a great task and musket balls were fired close to his head. His position was extremely perilous and he spurred his horse after the deserting soldiers. He came across a squadron of cavalry which looked lost and were awaiting orders. Hamilton waved his sword towards the Boyne, and urged his men into battle. He charged at their head back to the Boyne where Nassau had managed to come ashore.

Lord Antrim's Regiment was entangled with other troops and they also had panicked. The four Williamite regiments were securing themselves at the south bank as Hamilton returned to the attack with his cavalry. The Jacobites formed themselves against Nassau's troops. Some twenty cavalrymen had fallen under their horses under musket fire. The rest were carried off by the momentum of the charge and they swept along the riverbank and through the regiments of Caillemote and Cambron. Gustavus Hamilton's Enniskillen Regiment of Foot had now joined forces with William's Dutch Guards at Oldbridge. The east flank of these troops saw the banners of Richard Hamilton's cavalry fighting their way through the Huguenots. A volley of fire was sent up and the cavalry swept into action. There were sixty soldiers in the original squadron – only six to eight survived with Hamilton. They reached the main body of the Jacobite horse. Another attack was made against Nassau, and he was hard-pressed back into the Boyne. The two sides confronted each other across the river. Muskets were fired and pistols discharged. After a while Berwick's men started to advance.

The fighting here lasted about half an hour. There was nothing to be seen but dust and gunfire. Caillemote suffered heavily in this fight, himself receiving a wound. He was carried back across the Boyne. His men were demoralised and some of the soldiers wanted to desert. Just in time the Duke of Schomberg and his troops arrived, and he sized up the situation. He pulled out his sword and waved it at the advancing Jacobites. But now the regiment rallied, and he appealed to the Huguenot soldiers. The approach was successful. The Jacobite cavalry were now reinforced by Tyrconnel's regiment, with the Earl himself leading. Once again they were charging the Williamites. They were reinforced by Lord Galmoy's eight troops of fifty horse, which had been on the road to Rosnaree when they heard about the Oldbridge assault. They turned back, led now by the thirty-eight-year-old Pierce Butler, the third son of Viscount Galmoy, a cousin of the Williamite James Butler, Duke of Ormonde. Now that they were reinforced, the Jacobites made an impressive charge – their first charge yet.

The Danes had stated that it was the eleventh hour when William started to move, with a view to crossing the Boyne by Yellow Island. He wanted his infantry to cross first to establish a bridgehead. He left his three cavalry regiments under the command of his Major General of the Horse. The East Prussians were involved and John Ernst von Tettan had directed much of the engineering work on the campaign. Wurtemberg-Neustadt ordered the eight foot regiments across the river, himself at their head. He spearheaded his own Grand Regiment. The Danes were well armed, each soldier having the latest flintlock musket with a bayonet. The bayonets were used to great effect against the Jacobites. Each regiment's fittest men were promoted into grenadier companies, and armed with swords and hand grenades. The infantry officers and non-command officers carried half-pikes.

Wurtemberg-Neustadt said that the water was so deep that it came up to their armpits. They marched across by divisions, and the land was very boggy. Progress was slow and difficult and the enemy started to advance on the left flank of the Danes. Here were Berwick and Galmoy, backed by infantry regiments. The Danes hurried on across so that they should not be caught in midstream. In their hurry many of them found it difficult to get back to the ford. They found themselves up to their ears in water, trying to hold their muskets above their heads. But the Danes were able to reach the south bank before the Jacobites advanced. Wurtemberg-Neustadt said that while they were marching out of the water a squadron of dragoons arrived and attacked the guards. He allowed only the grenadiers and some platoons to charge, but the enemy repulsed them. As the Danes were trying to form up, many of them were not looking behind them until they had crossed the river again. Wurtemberg-Neustadt, by employing the bayonet, established a bridgehead. The Danes said that the enemy horse advanced, but they found the enemy vigorously firing. Wurtemberg-Neustadt said that the enemy forces would not attack again with their cavalry. The fighting had been rough, and an Irish soldier was captured. He thought that he had captured William himself. He was determined to take the Duke alive, but the commander of the Danish troops is said to have put him off until a Danish captain came up behind and pushed his sword into the Irishman's bowels.

Once the Danish bridgehead was secured, the main body of the Danish infantry started to cross. Now came the cavalry regiments and these were supported by the French and Dutch troopers. The Jacobites were now getting desperate, for the Williamites were wading their way through the waters. Still the Williamites had plenty in reserve, for they had not committed their dragoons or a large part of the cavalry. Tyrconnel tried to fend off the Williamite assault with a ferocious attack to which he committed all his cavalry. A thousand men charged down the slopes to Donore and made it to William's position from Oldbridge along the Boyne back to the east of Yellow Island. The Jacobites paid dearly, but William was full of admiration for James's efforts. Lieutenant General Douglas said that the enemy's force fought as bravely as any men could do, as they advanced towards him. The horse of Tyrconnel's Regiment acquitted themselves well, but the Dutch were like angels. Wurtemberg-Neustadt said that the Dutch fought so well that their infantry had enough time to save themselves. The Jacobite army was badly damaged in the charge of the cavalry of John Parker.

John Parker's family had been settled in Ireland for many years and an ancestor had been constable of Dublin Castle in 1453. His father had started his career as an excise officer; after a while he decided to become a doctor, opening a practice at Margate. He was made an honorary Fellow of the College of Physicians. His son, John, decided on a military career, being made captain of the Duke of York's Regiment. By 1687 he was a lieutenant colonel in the same regiment. The next year he followed James to France and then he left for Ireland. Four thousand men had fought in Parker's regiment in the charge against William, and only thirty men survived with their lives. Parker received a serious wound, and his lieutenant colonel and a major were killed. During the charge, Berwick's horse was killed under him. He had been sometimes surrounded by the enemy. With the support of him, his men could keep on fighting.

The charge killed many Jacobites; also the captain general of the Williamites had been killed, and all this time William's army was led by the eighty-four-year-old Duke of Schomberg. There were many casualties amongst the Williamites to start with. Defensive bayonets and pikes were sported. William's cavalry had not yet been committed at Oldbridge and here there was no way of counterattacking, so the Jacobite horse stood their ground. The use of the horse was apparent at this time. Douglas goes on further and remarked upon the inactivity of Schomberg's division facing James across the Boyne. At Oldbridge the people cried out, "Horse!

Horse!" This word described the forces, but they mistook it for another division. This stopped the right wing for about half an hour, and time was being lost for valuable service. A charge was made at Oldbridge about noon that day, and it arrived at where the Duke of Schomberg was commanding the Huguenot and Enniskillen regiments. He had received three sabre cuts over the head and one on the face, but it was a musket ball that struck him in the neck and tumbled him from his horse.

The Danish Ambassador informed his king that Schomberg had been struck in the neck by the bullet of a carbine. The shot threw the Duke from his horse, and he fell on a stony path. It was rumoured that the bullet was fired by a soldier near the Duke's side in Cambron's Regiment. The Jacobite claimed that Sir Cathal O'Toole of the Royal Regiment of Foot had recognised the Duke and shot him just before the Duke killed himself. The Duke died without uttering a word. A captain, who was near Schomberg, had been wounded in the arm, but he managed to dismount to help the Duke. The side movement also saw the death of George Walker of Siege of Londonderry fame. He was now the Bishop Designate of Londonderry, and he had been acting as chaplain to the Enniskillen regiments. He had gone to Schomberg's assistance when he was slain. However, this seems unlikely and it is more likely that he was fighting with Hamilton's Enniskillen Foot. He was wounded in the stomach, which killed him almost immediately. His body was stripped, for he was Scots Irish. When news of Walker's death reached William he said that he alas! joined the numbers that had fallen at the Boyne. William disliked fighting-priests. Walker's body was buried where he fell, by volunteers from Donoughmore. A little time afterwards, Walker's widow visited the site of his death. The body was disinterred and taken to Castlecaulfield, where he was finally laid to rest on the south side of the chancel in 1707.

Chapter 15

William in the Ascendant

Just before William heard about the death of the ex-Rector of Donoughmore and Governor of Londonderry, he had decided to cross the Boyne further downstream towards Drogheda, with dragoons and cavalry, so that he could encircle James, who was now delaying his advance. Godart van Ginkel was commander of his division. Ginkel was a veteran soldier, and had accompanied William to England in 1688. He had earned a ruthless reputation in capturing a Spanish regiment at Harwich when they declared themselves for James II. William directed Ginkel to take his Dutch cavalry regiment of 152 men, together with 258 soldiers of Sir Albert Conyngham's Dragoons, and the 241 men of Colonel Levison's Dragoons, so that they could find another crossing upstream. The Earl of Tyrconnel now saw William march up the river towards Donore. The regiment there had little experience. He rode along the crest of the hills of Rathmullen, always keeping William's men in sight; he would fight if the Jacobites tried to cross the Boyne. The Donore regiment eventually consisted of 400 men.

It was a good day, and the sun shone down upon the two kings, William of Orange and James II of England. The men were sweating and were powder-stained. At about this hour the Dutch Blue Guards started to march and began to ford the river at Oldbridge. At this time James's strength was outnumbered by William's soldiers by three to one.

William heard of the death of the Duke of Schomberg from one of the Duke's aides-de-camp. Clarke was always complaining about William's coldness, but to be sure William was not happy about the death of his general. He was sorry that the Duke had been slain by the Catholics. The death of the Duke might demoralise the troops so now William decided to cross the Boyne himself, to take part in the battle. William decided to follow Ginkel, and take the main body of his magnificent cavalry and the regiments of the Dutch Guards – at least 1,500 fresh troopers. They found that Ginkel was close to a bog. At this point the Boyne was deep and made even deeper by the displacement of water by the Williamite troops, already making their way across at Oldbridge, Grove Island and Yellow Island. The horses were not good at swimming. The ford was about a mile and a half from Oldbridge. Here a little stream emptied into the River Boyne from the north and a smaller steam also met the Boyne on the south bank. On the south bank the land rose to a height of one hundred feet within a few yards. A Huguenot cavalryman declared that he was the first to cross the Boyne with his cavalry. The news of Schomberg's death reached them just before they started to wade into the waters. There had been fresh fighting, and many officers and men had been slain. William eventually caught up with Ginkel as the crossing was in progress. On the other bank the Williamites observed Douglas's dragoons leaving the hills at Rathmullan to get nearer the water's edge to stop a crossing. William had ordered the two field guns to cover Ginkel. Some Danish foot soldiers were ordered to cross to give cover to the Dutch cavalry. Lord Dongan was killed by one of the cannon shots, and several of his soldiers were mowed down, killed or wounded. The two field guns and the muskets began to fire, and the rest of the regiment had to try to cross the hills in the Duleek direction. Some of the members of the regiment managed to retrieve the body of Douglas. They eventually carried it to Castletown, County Limerick, where he was given a soldier's funeral.

The opposition were now scattered. William started to cross the River Boyne himself. He was still clad in his finery, boasting the Star and Garter – an easy target for any Jacobite sniper. William's wound had caused much concern, and he could hardly lift a sword. He carried his sword in his left hand. The Danish Ambassador said that William arrived with nothing more than a walking stick, but the Ambassador was ever anxious to please his king.

William had difficulty in crossing. His horse soon became bogged down, and he had to dismount, and here his horse was dragged out of the mud. Tradition has it that it was an Enniskillener that volunteered to take the horse out of the mud, and so save his king. The crossing was very dangerous – William found it hard to walk three or four hundred paces before he was out of breath with his asthma. William, however, jumped back on the animal, and now the King was leading a total of nearly 2,000 cavalry, commanding his troops in encirclement movements towards Oldbridge. The remnent of Lord Douglas's Dragoons joined forces with the dragoon regiment of Viscount Clare. Clare's Regiment wore yellow uniforms, which earned them the title of 'The Yellow Dragoons'. This was the only regiment that stood between William and the unguarded right flank of the Jacobites. Clare mustered his dragoons and joined the Williamite forces. The Irish, it appeared, charged like madmen and the enemy regiment (probably Ginkel's Dutchmen) were driven back. It was rumoured that the Irish Army were drunk on brandy. Each man in the morning was issued with half a pint of the same. It seems that the front had not so great a position, and in the end the troops may not have been grateful for the alcohol. Brandy had been issued to the troops that March: the Jacobites made a rush to the barrels, and gave themselves plenty of drink. About 100 men were unfit for service and, as a result of the drink, many were left dead in the fields. It is difficult to ascertain what was going on at Oldbridge. William seems to have unjustly slighted Clare's Dragoons, saying that Clare had performed in a rude manner. The yellow-coat soldiers had fled, after the initial success of the first charge against Ginkel's cavalry. Clare was forced to fall back in good order. This left only Oliver O'Gara's regiment of foot soldiers facing the oncoming of the Williamite horse.

O'Gara's commanders were one William Mulloy and his seventeen-year-old nephew. Opposing the Jacobites was William Theobald, the father of Charles. Tradition had it that William Theobald presented his horse to King William when William's horse was shot. However, Charles was captured by the dragoons of his father's regiment. Because of Charles's age, William pardoned the boy and sent him home.

The Williamite cavalry were now across the Boyne in full strength; there seemed little hope for Jacobite resistance, and the Jacobite cavalry were starting to panic. The Jacobites now attempted to cross the Boyne. The Jacobite foot fell back, causing the infantry along the line from Drybridge to Oldbridge to follow suit. Many of them threw down their muskets and ran away. All that remained between William's war and the Jacobite's were the cavalry regiments of Tyrconnel and Sutherland and the thirty survivors from Parker's defeated Horse Guards. All that were left of the depleted Horse Guards were two troops. The Jacobites numbered less than 1,000 men, weary after two or three hours' fighting. They faced a victorious William with 15,000 troops, many of whom had not fired their muskets. The Jacobites charged and charged over again, and the Williamites could not understand their high morale. Ginkel had now recovered his lead in a charge along a lane that led to Oldbridge, along the banks of the Boyne on his way to Drogheda. The charge was now met by a Jacobite counterattack led by the well-known Dominick Sheldon, who turned Ginkel back. Ginkel did not like the idea of retreat and halted several yards down the lane, where the Jacobite cavalry were brought to a halt by Sheldon. Captain Brewerton, in command of five companies of Levison's Dragoons, was acting in concert with Ginkel on each side of the lane. Ginkel ordered his men to dismount and take up ambush positions in the hedges bordering the lane, ready for the charge of the Jacobites. Ginkel re-formed his Dutchmen and mounted another attack upon the Jacobite cavalry as they were returning down the lane. Sheldon had no time to make a horse charge, but urged his troops forward in the direction of Oldbridge. Ginkel was in hot pursuit and he said that the Jacobite troops were so close to them.

The Jacobites horse withdrew in good order, and William was consolidated on the south side of the Boyne. Percy Kirke had taken over Oldbridge with Henry Sidney, the colonel of William's English Foot Guards, as his second in command. William started to close in upon Donore from the east.

Tyrconnel saw the hopelessness of the situation and tried to make an orderly retreat to Duleek. He ordered Richard Hamilton to take command of the regiment and delay William as long as possible. Tyrconnel now left the field with Major General Dorrington in the wake of the fleeing Jacobites. Hamilton went back to Donore, and made a worthy defence, holding the Jacobite horse in close formation.

William raced forward, now that victory was within his grasp, and rode up to the nearest cavalry regiment, the Enniskilleners, commanded by the well-seasoned colonel, William Wolseley. He had been responsible for the Jacobite victory of 30 July 1689 at Newtownbutler, after he had defeated a force twice his strength. Wolseley said that his success was due to the quality of the men. Newtownbutler had given the Enniskilleners their name, and he urged that William should use them in the field. There were 423 men in the regiment. In the dust and smoke it was difficult to see the King. Several pistols had been aimed at him. Then Wolseley cried out that it was the King, for he was still sporting the Star and Garter. The Enniskilleners raised a cheer and William stood up in his stirrups, crying out that the Enniskilleners would be his guard today, and that he had heard much of them and wanted to see them in action. William led his men up the hill under tremendous fire from the Jacobites. William wanted the privilege of leading the Enniskilleners himself. He found that the men fought like a dream. William led his men up to the old ruined church at the top of the hill of Donore, where Hamilton had dismounted and dug in. In the heat it was impossible to tell friend from enemy. William was hit again – this time by two Jacobite musket balls, one of the shots hitting him in the back. It is said that William guarded the churchyard with his musketeers. The Enniskilleners made their attack against the walls of the church, at the same time as some Dutch troops made an assault on the south aisle. The Jacobites put up a fierce resistance at Donore. Hamilton said that if he remained at Donore, it would not be long before the Williamites would overthrow their position.

If the high ground at Donore was taken, the Oldbridge sector would become untenable for the Jacobites. The Williamites would pose a great threat to the Jacobite left. William also seems to have realised the position, for he had rejoined his Dutch Guards and was concentrating the whole attack on the hilltop. Hamilton retreated, his cavalry moving back to Platen Castle. The road ran south to Platen Castle and swung westwards to join the main Oldbridge-to-Duleek road. William was in hot pursuit before James had reached Platen. Hamilton had to draw up his cavalry once again and charge them. The Enniskilleners were routed by Hamilton. There were considerable casualties in the Williamite side. They broke their formation and fell back into the Danish cavalry of Colonel Monte Melchior von Dunop. Again there was confusion. Von Dunop confused the colonists with the Jacobite cavalry, who in turn thought that von Dunop's men were Jacobites. One man called out that he was about to kill as many Jacobites as possible, and then that he was an Enniskillener, wearing some green in his hat.

King Christian V was informed by the Danish Ambassador that the mission entrusted to him was now coming to an end. This was to support the efforts of King William.

Hamilton had joined Tyrconnel and the Jacobites in 1689, and a Williamite observer said that the 'papists' lit bonfires in celebration. They said that Hamilton was worth 10,000 men, and that he proved his worth during the Battle of the Boyne. Hamilton's brothers, Anthony and John, believed that their brother had been killed in the conflict. William led his men, despite his wounds, and was ready to meet Hamilton in the field. Hamilton was captured and some days later he was transferred to the Tower of London. He was at length exchanged for the Williamite William Stewart, 1st Viscount Stewart, who had been imprisoned in the Bastille the previous year.

The Duke of Berwick was the first in command of the Jacobite cavalry whilst Hamilton was indisposed. He regrouped his forces and led them slowly past the plateau. He swung westwards to command the main road to Duleek. The Jacobites were confident with the original 1,000 troopers. It was impossible that the Jacobites could now defeat William. The task for the Jacobites was that they should be led to Duleek in safety.

Chapter 16

On the Eve of James's Retreat

It was just after two o'clock when a messenger brought the news that the enemy had forced the pass at Oldbridge and that the right flank was defeated. James now realised that he had made a mistake by moving two thirds of this army to the left. The Williamites had left Oldbridge too weakly protected. There was only one way to bring matters to a conclusion: he told Lauzun that there was little time to waste and an attack by the Williamites was a great priority, but the opportunity was lost. The Marquis de la Hoguette was ordered to take command of the French troops, to act as a vanguard in the event of an attack by Count Schomberg. The dragoons were given the order to dismount and have their muskets at the ready. The dragoon regiments were led by Robert Clifford, Francis Carroll and Thomas Maxwell. Excitement moved across the soldiers. There had been long periods of waiting, but now a real battle was about to begin. The Jacobites had started to move. James's informers had now learnt that it was impossible for the horse to charge the enemy. A ditch had been made to thwart a cavalry attack. James, as usual, dithered. The Jacobite troops were now impatient and were anxious to start a charge. Valuable time was being lost. Lauzun said that the deep narrow gorge and bog prevented James from closing with the enemy. The Marquis Lery de Girardin confirmed that it was impossible to organise a charge against the enemy over such poor terrain. However, some believed that the French and Irish troops were evenly matched. The Jacobites were now in a position to either give up the struggle or wait to be beaten.

There was little possibility of the Jacobites beating William. Military reputations were now made on the Protestant side and were recorded in accounts of the Battle of the Boyne. James now wanted to see some action.

Sarsfield had been born at Lucan, near Dublin, about 1650, an offspring of the old English families who had arrived in Ireland as standard bearers to Henry II. His wife, Anne, was the daughter of an Irishman who had led the 1641 uprising of Catholics versus Protestants. Sarsfield was a devout Catholic. In September 1681 he had challenged Lord Grey to a duel for denigrating the Gaels. Sarsfield was educated at a French military academy and then commissioned in the English Army as a captain in Colonel Douglas's regiment of foot in 1678. He now helped Tyrconnel to get rid of Protestants in high positions in Ireland, and he helped to remodel the Irish Army. Sarsfield had been born in England. He followed James to France and later to Ireland, where he was given command of his own regiment and made a privy counsellor. He had also served in the Irish parliament, being returned for Dublin. He was not well disposed to the Crown's servants. However, he was marked out as a competent commander. He was full of courage and tenacity. He did not like the idea of inactivity that morning. Tom Maxwell was on the record as being in a very good mood for attacking the enemy. De la Hoguette criticised Sarsfield. He said the terrain was only an excuse for not closing with Schomberg, but this may not have been true.

The situation suddenly came out of the hands of the Jacobite generals. James records that, at the same time as the dragoons got on horseback, the whole line began to march by their flank to the right. The Jacobites soon lost sight of their own men because of a village that interposed. There was a considerable cloud of dust as the Jacobites and the Williamites advanced. Count Schomberg and his lieutenant general thrashed the Jacobites and hemmed them in in a joint action. The Jacobite position would become increasingly perilous. Berwick informed the King of the situation. William had now forced the passage at Oldbridge. William caused his troops to march by the left for Duleek. Berwick probably referred to a river in the region.

Lauzun ordered his troops to march off by the left flank towards Dublin. James had been left looking across the bog towards the dust of the Williamite army marching southwards. Lauzun now started to panic but still urged his cavalry on. De la Hoguette agreed with him and pointed out that this would put the Jacobite infantry in grave danger. Lauzun replied that the main priority was saving James himself, who now started to accept defeat and eventual exile. He ordered that de la Hoguette was not to lose contact with the Williamite forces. Sarsfield's Regiment was to act as an escort. The Jacobite army was now on a collision course. Both armies were now heading for the same river crossing on the small riverbank at the village of Duleek. James found it hard to justify such a policy of defeat, saying that the high bog dictated strategy. The river was impassible except at Duleek. The Jacobite left could have retreated along the main road to Slane in good order without becoming embroiled with the retreating Duke of Tyrconnel, Richard Talbot.

The Grand Prior's Regiment was waiting for the order to engage Count Schomberg. They clearly knew that Oldbridge was under attack, but the enemy had been beaten by Lord Douglas, who was killed. The regiment was in good spirits, vigorous and desirous of battle. One thousand strong, they appeared to be invincible. Now came the surprising order to retreat towards Duleek. The Grand Prior's Regiment turned and began to march towards Duleek 'Lane', which was a road with high banks. The regiment was marching ten abreast and in good order. A group of Jacobite horse had fled down the lane. They broke the whole line of foot, riding through the Jacobite battalions. The horse came with great speed, some firing their muskets.

The object was to control the situation. Few men could be seen, but with order and leadership they would stand together and repair the colours. Some threw away their arms, others their coats and shoes, so that they could more easily run. It was still possible to see the hills, and they were covered with soldiers of several regiments, scattered like sheep and flying before the Williamite 'wolves'. Now followed all the tragedy and defeat of the Jacobite forces. Schomberg now realised that the enemy was in full retreat. News came from Oldbridge that the Williamites were now in pursuit of the overthrown Jacobite forces. Sir John Dalrymple said that the Count pursued slowly from Oldbridge. He was now of course familiar with the bogs and ditches, so that the forces could easily move forward. Schomberg was now certain that William would win the day. The Danish Ambassador informed Christian V that the pincer movement, which was to encircle the entire Jacobite army, did not come about because of the Count's immobility in the bog. Instead of mobilisation it would have been more effective for Schomberg and Douglas to take the road from Slane towards Dublin. According to James this is what had happened when he gave the order to retire to Duleek. The Danish Ambassador pointed out that Schomberg had no orders to cut off the Jacobite retreat, and William did not pursue James as efficiently as he could. Schomberg's cavalry had formed itself into one body and Oldbridge had been easily taken at about nine or ten in the evening. The hills that surrounded the plain, where both armies had been encamped, favoured James's flight. The Williamite cavalry were exhausted after a twelve-hour march. Whilst William was in pursuit of James, both columns of infantry were marching in good order. This action was a rout rather than a battle. The loss of lives was perhaps great on both sides.

The Jacobites said that it was the sight of their army retreating in good order that prompted William not to pursue the overthrown James. The position of the troops allowed the Jacobites to retreat in an orderly manner. Bishop Burnet gave a more perceptive account of the policies of William. After James's army had disintegrated, William was of the opinion that the Irish would surrender. A speedy retreat would have been a dignified retreat, and he always had a fear of that. Burnet was of the opinion that extreme views about the situation should not be heard. Bentinck was of the opinion that muskets be given to each of the 3,000 cavalry troops to pursue the Jacobites, but William was not keen on the proposal. Jacobites that had fallen into the hands of the Williamites were shown no mercy. Few of the men that had escaped came into William's hands, for the Jacobites were shot like hares amongst the corn and in the hedges as they retreated.

According to Stevens, the regiments of Louis XIV of France conducted an honourable retreat, taking away the cannon and marching smartly after the shock of defeat. The French, however, were never committed throughout the entire campaign. Lauzun and de la Hoguette were later accused of cowardice. Stevens pursued the Blue Regiment of Conrad von Zurlauben. The retreat of the Jacobites from Oldbridge ran into the Williamite forces, who collided with the Jacobite troops from Rosnaree. There were bogs and ditches just before Duleek, with high banks on both sides. There was only one place to cross, where six men could march abreast. De la Hoguette wrote from Kinsale on 14 July, trying to put the blame on the Irish troops for the collision. The troops were not only beaten, but they were driven before the Williamites like sheep. It is true to say that poor leadership had led to James's defeat and his flight to the French court. Three days later de la Hoguette gave perhaps a more true account: he said that Tyrconnel had retired in good order. Now confusion had well and truly broken out.

Others were more frank. In those regiments comprised mainly of German and Swiss, the King's service was praised. Colonel Conrad von Zurlauben said that he would expose the faults which were the reasons for losing the battle. He claimed that Lauzun, de la Hoguette and others had abandoned them. Zurlauben said that the officers put regimental colours in their pockets and left the battlefield. His regiment, hailed by the Catholics, made a retreat. The infantry retreat from Oldbridge and the troops from Rosnaree reached Duleek at the same time. Zurlauben had reported that he was forced to fire on the panic-stricken soldiers to stop them destroying the formations of his men. They were then able to draw up on the high ground beyond the Duleek crossing. Louis XIV had very little time for the troops that had fought at the Boyne, except perhaps Zurlauben – the only one mentioned at Versailles to receive Louis's thanks.

Berwick was still retreating towards Duleek with his cavalry from Oldbridge – the last of the Jacobite troops to leave the Boyne scene. He wrote that a detachment of the enemy followed them. They stopped at a narrow pass and the enemy did the same. He said that they were glad that they had built a bridge: Berwick echoed the words of the Danish Ambassador, de la Fouleresse. Marshal Schomberg had died, and he had fallen in hand-to-hand fighting at Oldbridge. Schomberg, it is recorded, was a better general than the Prince of Orange. The Jacobites were allowed to retreat peacefully.

Duleek had been the scene of the aftermath of the Boyne: Brian Boru, High King of Ireland, had been slain at the Battle of Clontarf in 1014; his body was brought to Duleek Abbey in the Boyne Valley at the point of a sword. Duleek Abbey was founded in 488 by St Ciaran. The body of the High King and his son were taken to Louth.

Berwick came up with his cavalry, just as the last of the King's troops were passing the brook. Those troops of the Prince of Orange which kept advancing arrived at the same time. He was obliged to pass the defile at full speed. The entire army was drawn up and ready for battle. The enemy did the same opposite to the Williamites, but they did not attack. The Jacobites retreated another seven miles towards Naul. Most of James's troops were without direction from the general officers. However, discipline was still held: 6,000 French troops made a brave retreat, fighting and marching by day and night until they arrived at Dublin. The pride of the Jacobite infantry was now gathered into a disciplined force by Brigadier John Wauchope, in whose brigade it had originally been. Stevens said that he, being the eldest, should command the division. As they marched on, the panicking soldiers began to disperse. The Jacobites dispersed in such a manner that William could hardly keep pace with them. Wanderers from other regiments started to join in the battle, amongst them some of the dragoons. The soldiers were in good order, though some had lost their weapons, and others their coats, hats and shoes.

Berwick now emerged as the most senior officer and he took command of the retreating troops. Five miles from Dublin he ordered a rest for the troops in some fields. Stevens said that grief was not the only burden he had to bear. They had been marching from three o'clock in the morning until dusk, in the great heat of the sun. They had great thirst – a thirst that could not be quenched by drinking from a puddle. Near Duleek, and behind them, some Jacobite artillery was still firing. It was poorly manned by the French, who brought it into action against William, now in hot pursuit. They fired for one and a half hours using small shot, which fell very thick upon the Williamites, who had hidden partly in the bushes.

Bellingham had accompanied William and his Dutch cavalry almost as far as Naul. It was ten o'clock, and dusk was closing in. He acted as guide to William, back to the village of Duleek, and left him there. He said that he had returned to Oldbridge. The King slept in his coach at Duleek, where he spent the night. He was faint as a result of his efforts and wanted drink and meat. Story says that the Jacobites were in confusion and they left a considerable amount of ammunition in the village and, indeed, all over the countryside. Story also says that his men were so foolish as to blow up the powder wherever they came across it. James's belongings were found at Duleek. This should have been enough to quash the rumours that King James had planned to flee before the battle, and that a ship had been found for him the evening before the battle, for James was now sure that he should leave Ireland. Williamite propaganda had painted a portrait of James in flight, just as soon as he had landed in the north. This was a ridiculous rumour but eagerly accepted by the Williamites. The Williamites found baggage, gold watches and a silver dinner service, as well as some pikes, said to be between 4,000 and 5,000, which the soldiers burnt to keep themselves warm. It was a chilly night. Some of Tyrconnel's papers were captured, and when they were examined it was found that there was an assassination plot against William. Tyrconnel wrote to Mary of Modena at St Germain and considered the Jacobite cause as having been lost. Burnet said that the Marquis was an Irishman who had served under the Bourbons and he had been chosen to assassinate William. Sir Robert Southwell had provided Burnet with copies of the letters he found in Tyrconnel's baggage. Tories, a pseudonym for an Irish soldier, had arrived in Ireland from France but was calling a tune for his services. In another letter Tyrconnel was supposed to have discussed the plot with James, who at first did not like the idea. There is no evidence that James was ever in a mind to assassinate William. With James's flight to France, the Battle of the Boyne was over.

William retired to his carriage, which he frequented during the Irish campaign. It was designed by Sir Christopher Wren. He congratulated the Duke of Wurtemburg-Neustadt on the bravery of those in his command. William made sure that the Danish Ambassador reported this act in his next letter to Christian V. This would help Christian to maintain in command of the Danish troops in William's service. William next consoled Schomberg on the death of his father. William said that he owed much to Schomberg for his support at the Boyne. Most of William's officers lay in the fields with their men. It was dark and the Williamites had to put up with the field during the night. George Clarke, the Secretary of War (who had attached himself to some of the dragoons chasing the Jacobite cavalry), said that they would sleep on the ground. The Williamites now rounded up more of the Jacobites. The fight was over for the Danish Ambassador, and it was now James's intention to collect together the remains of his army before the gates of Dublin. The Williamites would try to oppose James, and at length the Jacobites gave up the struggle to capture the Irish capital. Bellingham rode back to the camp at Oldbridge. He was exhausted but happy.

Chapter 17

Conclusion

The Glorious Revolution of 1688 produced the events that took place in Ireland. The Convention Parliament had formulated the Settlement of 1689 and its future remained uncertain until James was defeated in the field and order restored throughout the British Isles. There were more casualties at the Battle of Aughrim (1691). It was the outcome of the Boyne that set James on a course of flight from his kingdom. William was now able to turn his attention back to Europe. The Battle of the Boyne and the 1688 Revolution have been derided 300 years later by those opposed to the influences produced by them. In the nineteenth century, liberals and Loyalists looked back to the events of 1690 proclaiming that William's stand at the Boyne was a victory for democracy. The Glorious Revolution was seen as having a meaning, taking place with scheming and plotting. James was overthrown and William realised his ambitions. The Battle of the Boyne became a minor second-rate battle hardly worth mentioning. The degrading of the Boyne has come about over the last three decades by the so-called efforts to destroy Ulster in favour of a united Ireland and for the sake of the Roman Catholic Church. The Loyalists were aware that there were those who wanted to debase the memory of this great battle – truly a 'Glorious, Pious and Immortal Memory'.

The Battle of the Boyne has been dismissed as a mere skirmish, a fight between a small number of forces, but this is not the case. William III commanded at the Boyne 45,000 men (35,000 infantry and 10,000 cavalry). He engaged James, who had 35,000 men (25,000 infantry and 10,000 cavalry). The two armies were not equal. William had a great number of troops compared with other battles of the period. The French General Condé commanded 40,000 men against William in Europe in 1674, whilst Marlborough commanded 52,000 at Blenheim in 1704. The Battle of the Boyne was a long drawn-out affair, typical of a full-scale battle. The opening shots had been fired at Rosnaree at 8 a.m. and the pursuit of the fleeing enemy lasted to about 10 p.m., a period of about fourteen hours. William himself was in the saddle for up to seventeen hours. The main attack had been at Oldbridge, where there was a major assault across the River Boyne. The troops were faced with heavy fire until William brought in the cavalry to their assistance and conducted the final advance against the Jacobite position on the hill of Donore. The Williamite soldiers were heavily criticised for their unsoldierly activity.

King William has been accused of being a poor general, making errors which limited the success of his campaign. It is difficult to accept these criticisms when the facts are considered. William had been thrown into military service at twenty-one years of age, in 1672, when the French had invaded the United Provinces. With disaster looming, the Dutch turned to the struggle of the House of Orange. William's determination rallied the Dutch, but William declared that he had not much training in the arts of war. He reformed the Dutch Army, and the French were driven out of the Netherlands in 1678. William had the inferior numbers, and the French commanders, Luxembourg and Condé, withdrew under cover of darkness, leaving the wounded on the battlefield. Good commanders are judged by the men they lead. Soldiers who respect and admire their commander have confidence in him. A good relationship between a commander and his men make a formidable fighting force, the mystical bond between the led and the leader. A poor commander cannot command such devotion. The force that marched into the Boyne Valley on 30 June 1690 was in a high state of morale because of the prestige of King William.

William's forces were the pride of England and the House of Orange, and included English; Scots; Dutch; Germans; Danes; French Huguenot refugees fleeing from religious persecution;, and English Scots settlers from Ireland, mainly from Ulster. Some of the men fought for their religion;, some for the homeland; the English and Scots for the Revolution and the Constitutional Settlement. Many were mercenaries, professional soldiers that enjoyed the military life for as long as the generals paid them. The same problems surrounded James's army. William was the absolute commander and he had grown accustomed to the French-Dutch War. He had observed the Jacobite position on 30 June in the morning and said that he was glad to rely on his commanders.

He ordered the troops to camp where trees prevented the Jacobites from accurately assessing their numbers and composition. William and his staff rode to the banks of the Boyne to ascertain the enemy's position. William sat, having a picnic lunch and enjoying his success vis-à-vis the senior Jacobite position. The Jacobites brought up two cannon to be concealed by the south banks. William and his men remounted. Now the cannon were fired. The first shot killed the horse of Georg of Daamstadt, and William expressed his grief. But the second shot hit William on the right shoulder and he fell forward in the saddle. A great cheer rose from the Jacobites, and news was sent to Louis XIV and the Pope with the great news of William's death. Some of William's staff thought that he had been killed but William was upright and his troops regained their enthusiasm. William exclaimed, "Thank God it came not closer!" A field dressing was applied to the wound. His officers crowded round to express their grief and hope. The King exclaimed that his commander should not move on. The troops now sang 'God Save the King'. By dusk William had planned his strategy, but no record of his tactics were made. It would have been unwise of him to have done so. The opening of the battle was to be a feint with the right wing.

Count Schomberg was to force a passage with 10,000 men. The enemy's position was closer to his left. Schomberg's men spearheaded the crack regiments of the army to force a passage at Oldbridge. This would tie down the bulk of the Jacobite forces and further disguise William's intention. William always positioned himself where the fighting was heaviest. He would lead his cavalry across the river on the left flank and so swing round into the enemy's right and rear, thus destroying James's army. It has been suggested that King William faced his Waterloo at the Boyne, but history proves otherwise.

At dawn on 1 July, Count Schomberg led his division to the ford of Rosnaree. The first crossing took place with 800 dragoons. The forcing of the River Boyne at Rosnaree was mistaken for the main Orange attack. At about 10.15 a.m., before the line of the Jacobites, Schomberg commanded the famous Blue Guards, William's elite regiment, to cross the Boyne. Their drums were beating the forerunner of the lambeg drum. They thundered out across the river and the Guards waded towards the southern bank.

At approximately 11 a.m. Schomberg ordered the French Huguenots in support of the Guard's left. They reached the southern bank of the river and their commander was hit by a musket ball. The troops faltered. Schomberg rushed to the head of the column and pointed with his sword to a French regiment. He shouted out that they should surrender and that there would be no persecution. He was cut to pieces by a group of about five of James's cavalry. As we have seen, the hero of Londonderry, George Walker, was killed while rushing to his aid. Now William is reputed to have said, "My poor Guards! My poor Guards!" William, informed of Schomberg's death, now ordered Ginkel to lead the cavalry across the river on the left wing. Ginkel now tried to cross the Boyne at the ford at Drybridge. William rode to the left and prepared the cavalry to cross. His assault was only slightly opposed: the bulk of the Jacobite cavalry by now were committed to the counterattack at Oldbridge. The Williamite cavalry had reached the south bank, after wading deeply in the water; they now headed to the Oldbridge sector to support the infantry. The Jacobites fell back to the hill of Donore, and William encouraged the

Enniskillen foot and dragoons. In the dust they did not recognise the person of William on his white horse. One dragoon pointed his pistol at William's head. He pushed it away and proclaimed what the Enniskilleners could do for him. The King was alive! and his chase of the Jacobites would be complete. A trooper admired the King's bravery: "Anything Your Majesty may desire."

The remaining Jacobites now held strong at the hill of Donore, a mile up the Boyne and their position was becoming more and more precarious. A large number of the Irish infantry had fled. The cavalry had been committed and its effectiveness thereby reduced as a result of the casualties and fatigue. The main obstacle, the River Boyne, had now been lost to William. The remaining infantry and assault cavalry squadron occupied the hill of Donore. This had been fortified but could easily be outflanked on either side. Before the Jacobites were the Williamite forces that had driven them back from the River Boyne. Schomberg's forces, now reinforced, threatened the left and rear of the Donore position. The hill of Donore lay beyond the Jacobite camp, and now the Orange forces had already captured James's baggage, tents and supplies. It was now rumoured that James was on the retreat towards Dublin and this demoralised the Jacobites. As Patrick Sarsfield later remarked on being captured: "Exchange kings with me and we will fight you again."

William, with all his brushes with death, seemed to lead a charmed life. One bullet had shot off the cap of his pistol as he crossed the Boyne and another grazed his boot. After about an hour's fighting the Williamites were in possession of the hill. Schomberg, seeing that King William was victorious and threatening the rear of the Jacobites facing him, moved to the right to cut off their retreat by a pincer movement. Lauzun now ordered a full retreat of the remnants of James's France-Irish army.

The Williamite cavalry pursued the enemy south, but the infantry were too exhausted to join in and the cavalry were too tired to gallop. The Irish infantry had left the battlefield when the Orange troops had crossed at Oldbridge between 10 a.m. and noon. Ginkel wrote that the Jacobites ran so fast that his forces could not keep up with them. The victory was complete, the Revolution Settlement secured and the memory glorious.

Today, many think that the Battle of the Boyne was but a skirmish, and not part of a religious war. However, religion was one of the causes of the war in Ireland. James II had two clear objectives and great ambition. The first was to claim absolute power for the Crown, the second was to pave the way for the return of his kingdom to Roman Catholicism. He asserted that no one could hold office under him if he were a Protestant. By 1688 he was proposing to Louis XIV an alliance between England and France to destroy heresy everywhere. The survival of Protestantism in England, Scotland and Wales depended upon James being ousted from the throne and the impossibility of his restoration.

Louis had repealed the Edict of Nantes, which had guaranteed religious toleration in France, but his Huguenot subjects were driven into exile. The survival of Protestantism in Europe depended upon curtailing Louis XIV's ambitions. William was a profoundly religious person. He had been brought up as a Calvinist from a young age, and he trusted in God to guide him. These were the figures that had been involved in the war – James, Louis and William – but it was William that was the most religious, though he was not a bigot. It was the policy of Louis XIV which drove the Catholic Roman Emperor and King of Spain into alliance with Protestant William. It was William's ambition that held the realm together in the face of the Jacobite threat. It was rumoured that William was supported by the Pope. The papacy seemed to remain neutral in a divided Europe. Open support of William would alienate Catholic forces on the Continent. Louis was urged to curb his anti-clerical policies of 1688. James, before the battle, was in contact with the Pope and wrote that 'The only reason for all these rebellions against us is that we have remained faithfully to the true religion.' Religion was a leading issue in the war. Some take the view that Protestantism should not have survived; they look back at the Battle of the Boyne as a symbol not only of military defeat but the triumph of Protestantism.

King William's victory at the Boyne today is celebrated on 12 July. However, fortune might have reverted the victory at the Boyne. William and Mary remained on the throne, and parliament continued the process of government. Parliament was freely elected and had the right to criticise the Crown's policies. James was an autocrat. The law courts maintained their independence, which James had denied. The political nation now demanded the right to be consulted regarding policy and could refuse consent to that policy. The foundation of modern democracy was made at the Boyne. The battle seemed to establish an unwritten British constitution and to reinforce the Glorious Revolution. The Battle of the Boyne is well remembered and has been described as glorious. Some Protestants in Ulster today cry out to Roman Catholics – "Remember 1690!"

Select Bibliography

Stephen B. Baxter, *William III* (Longmans, 1966)

Hilaire Belloc, *James II*

Peter Bereford Ellis, *The Boyne Water* (Blackstaff, 1989)

Cecil Kilpatrick, *William of Orange* (Grand Orange Lodge of Ireland, 1998)

Lucy Elaine McClure Gordon, *The Twelfth* (Ulster Society, 1997)

Enda O'Boyle, *The Battle of the Boyne*

Robert Shephard, *Ireland, Its Fate – The Boyne and After* (Aurum Press, 1990)

Padraig Lenihan, *The Battle of the Boyne* (Tempus Publishing, 2003)

John Kinross, *The Boyne and Aughrim* (The Windrush Press)

Robert Wallace, *King William III and the Battle of the Boyne* (Grand Orange Lodge of Ireland, 1989)